Sacrifice Kicks

Flying, Hopping, Jumping and Suicide Kicks

Advanced Martial Arts Kicks for Realistic Airborne Attacks

from Karate, Kung Fu, Krav Maga, Tae Kwon Do, MMA, Muay Thai, Capoeira and more

By

Marc De Bremaeker

Fons Sapientiae Publishing

Sacrifice Kicks – Flying, Hopping, Jumping and Suicide Kicks. Published in 2016 by Fons Sapientiae Publishing, Cambridge, United Kingdom

ISBN: 978-0-9934964-7-9

Recommended reading, by the same author:

"Stealth Kicks - The Forgotten Art of Ghost Kicking" (2015)
"Ground Kicks-Advanced Martial Arts Kicks for Goundfighting" (2015)
"Stop Kicks-Jamming, Obstructing, Stopping, Impaling, Cutting and Preemptive Kicks" (2014)
"Low kicks-Advanced Martial Arts Kicks for Attacking the Lower Gates" (2013)
"Plyo-Flex-Plyometrics and Flexibility Training for Explosive Martial Arts Kicks" (2013)
"The Essential Book of Martial Arts Kicks" (2010) by Tuttle Publishing
"Le Grand Livre des Coups de Pied" (2016) by Budo Edition (In French)
"i Calci nelle Arti Marziali" (2015) by Edizioni Mediterranee (in Italian)

DEDICATION

To my grandchildren, the apples of my eyes...

Family is not an important thing. It's everything.
~Michael J. Fox

Dear Reader,

In this day and age, the life of a serious author has become quite difficult. The proliferation of books and the explosion of internet content has made it nearly impossible to promote work based on extensive research and requiring complex lay-out.
Please enjoy this book. Once you are finished, I would ask kindly that you take a few short minutes to give your honest opinion. A unbiased Amazon review, of even a few words only, would be highly appreciated and encouraging.

Thank You,

Marc

Nothing is ever lost by courtesy. It is the cheapest of pleasures, costs nothing, and conveys much.
~Erastus Wiman

ACKNOWLEDGEMENTS

Without the active support of my wife and life companion, *Aviva Giveoni*, this book would not have come to life. Being an athlete in her own right, she understands the meaning of hard work and dedication.

Aviva

Sensei Shlomo Faige

Among many teachers and heads and shoulders above, my late Sensei, -*Sidney (Shlomo) Faige*-, should be mentioned with longing thankfulness. Sensei Faige founded the Shi-Heun style of Karate.

Special Thanks to my life-long friend and training partner, *Roy Faige*, for his help and support. Roy is now heading the Shi Heun school is also my co-author of *The Essential Book of Martial Arts Kicks*. His influence and advice is felt in nearly every page of this work and the previous books in the series.

Roy and Marc

Darren and Joey

Thank you to *Ziv Faige, Gil Faige, Shay Levy, Dotan De Bremaeker, Nimrod De Bremaeker, Joey Grotyohann, Darren Grotyohann and Itay Leibovitch* who helped by painstakingly posing for some of the photographs.

Most photographs have been taken by the author, by Roy Faige and by Aviva Giveoni. But special thanks have to be extended to talented *Grace Wong* for some long sessions. Thank you also to professional photographer *Guli Cohen*: some of the photographs in this book have been extracted from the photo sessions he gracefully did for previous volumes.

The drawings in this book are mine. Everything that I have learned about line art, I have done so from professional Illustrator *Shahar Navot*, who illustrated *The Essential Book of Martial Arts Kicks*. Thanks Shahar!

A lifetime of training for just ten seconds.
~Jesse Owens

CONTENTS

Foreword to the "Kicks" Series

A goal is not always meant to be reached, it often serves simply as something to aim at.
~Bruce Lee

The 'Foreword' and 'General Introduction' are very similar to those of the previous book in the 'Kicks' series. In order to spare a near re-read to our faithful readers of 'Low Kicks', 'Stop Kicks', 'Ground Kicks' and 'Stealth Kicks', we invite you to go directly to the 'Introduction to Sacrifice Kicks' on page xx.

My Martial Arts career started with Judo at age 6. Judo was pretty new Fifty years ago, and a bit mystical in the Western World. A mysterious Oriental Art teaching how to use one's opponent's strength against him was a pretty attractive proposition for a wimpy kid. And the decorum and costume trappings made it a unique selling proposition. That is, until the Kung Fu craze of the Seventies, starring Bruce Lee, and then others.
In my opinion, what fascinated the Western masses, and the teen-ager I was then, was mostly the fantastic kicking maneuvers in the spectacular fights of those Kung-Fu movies. The bulk of the fight scenes were based on spectacular exchanges, the likes of which we had never seen before. What was new and revolutionary back then, may seem banal and common to today's younger reader. But we had been raised in the era of boxing and we had been conditioned by the fair-play of *Queensburry's* rules: we had no idea one could fight *like that*!
It was also the first time that the general public in Europe and America had seen a well-rounded Martial Art in action: punching, but also striking, kicking, throwing down, grappling, locking... It comprised all fighting disciplines in seamless aggregation. Wow! Judo was great, but I now wanted to *kick* like Bruce Lee. I therefore took up *Shotokan Karate*. 'Shotokan-ryu' is not the most impressive kicking style, but it was then the most developed Kicking Art outside of Asia and the only one available to me. It is as well and I certainly do not regret it. Though it is not an art known for extravagant kicks, Shotokan is very well organized didactically. It also emphasizes tradition, hard training, focus (*Zanshin*) and mastery of basic work. In all athletic endeavors, the continuous drilling of basic work at all levels of proficiency is the only real secret to success.

...And traditional Shotokan Karate drills and low training stances definitely fit this bill. So, during the whole of my career, I kept practicing Shotokan Karate, or a Shotokan-derived style at all times. I also kept at Judo, my first love. But in parallel, I started to explore other Arts a few years at the time, as opportunities and geography allowed. During my long Martial Arts career, I also did practice assiduously Karatedo from the *Kyokushinkai*, *Shotokai*, *Wadoryu* and *Sankukai* schools. I also trained for long stints of *TaeKwonDo*, *Muay Thai*, *Krav Maga*, *Capoeira*, *Savate-Boxe Française*, two styles of traditional *Ju-Jitsu* and some soft styles of *Kung Fu*. This search is where I developed my individual methods and my own understanding of the Art of Kicking and its place in complex fighting. It also provided the basis on which to build my own personal research. Of course, this is strongly accented towards the type of maneuvers and training that favor my personal physiology and personality, but I have tried very hard to keep an open mind, among others through coaching.

Sometimes during this maybe too eclectic career, my travels took me to the **Shi-Heun** School of the late *Sensei Sidney Faige*, mentioned in the Acknowledgements. The *Shi-Heun* style is *Shotokan*-derived and mixed with *Judo* practice. It emphasizes extreme conditioning, total fighting under several realistic rules sets and the personal quest for what works best for oneself. And its self-defense training is based on no-nonsense *Krav Maga*. As

Sensei Sidney Faige in action

this was only the early Eighties, this was definitely a prophetic ancestor of today's phenomena of Mixed Martial Arts of 'UFC' fame. The free-fighting rules in the *Dojo* were 'all-out' and 'to-the-ground', but this did not hinder the success of the School's students in more traditional tournaments under milder rules. The direct disciples of *Sensei Faige* did indeed roam the tournament scene undefeated for years.

In these days, points tournament fighting was mainly WUKO (World Union of Karate

Sensei Faige with the winning Israeli National Team; the author and Roy Faige are on the right

Organizations), with some notable exceptions like *Kyokushinkai* and *Semi-contact Karate* bouts. Unfortunately, WUKO generally (boringly) consisted in two competitors safely jumping up-and-down and waiting for the other to initiate a move, in order to stop-reverse-punch him to the body.

When my name was called up in these events, there was usually some spontaneous applause from the spectators; they knew they were going to see, finally, some kicking. I apologize if it sounds like boasting; the point I am trying to make is that Karate fans of these times came to see kicking and rich fighting moves, and not some unrealistic form of boxing. And this is not to denigrate *Karatedo*, but more to critisize the castrating effect of unintelligent rules sets.

Marc and Roy facing off at the finals of a 1987 Points Tournament

Marc, kicking in point tournament

…It is my strong belief that Kicking is what made the Oriental Martial arts so appealing. As I have already mentioned in articles and previous books, I do firmly argue that *kicking is more effective than punching.* This usually causes many to stand up, disagree and maybe want to *punch* me, pun intended. This is an old debate, still raging, and I respectfully ask to be allowed to complete the sentence. I strongly believe that kicking is more effective than punching, **but proficiency takes much more time and work**. When presented this way, I do hope that this opinion is more acceptable to most. Let me detail my position briefly.

Kicking is more efficient than punching:

1. Because of the longer range

2. Because the muscles of the leg are much bigger and powerful than those of the arms

3. Because kicking targets, unlike punching targets, go from head all the way down to toes

4. Because kicks are less expected and therefore more surprising than punches, especially at shorter ranges

One needs to drill kicks from very close ranges as well

I readily admit that the opponents of my position do have valid arguments. They will point out that kicks are inherently slower than punches and can be easily jammed because they start from longer ranges. They will also point out that kicking often opens the groin, while forgetting that so does punching usually as well. It is my experience that, - *after a lot of dedicated and intelligent work-,* many kicks can be *as swift as punches and can be delivered at all ranges and from all positions.*

...During all my training years, I invested a lot of time, personal drilling and original research into Kicking Arts from all over the world. I experimented with all training tips gathered and I endeavored to try all mastered new kick variations in actual free-fighting and competitive tournaments. Here is the place to note that this is *not* about a huge number of different techniques; it is about finding the best possible techniques suited to one's specific strength, physiology and affinities (Once you have found your **few** techniques and the best way to drill them, then you focus on a fast and perfect execution from all ranges and positions). During my quest in the realm of kicking, I slowly developed a personal kicking style based on my personal history and mindset. I researched most of the available literature, but very few treatises were actually *dedicated* to kicking. The few works I found about kicking were generally very good, but usually style-restricted and unorganized. I never found the kind of book that I would have liked to have at the start of my Martial arts career. And so I decided to write it myself and share my global view of the subject. To the best of my knowledge, there has never been an attempt to compile and organize all the different Kick types and variation in such a way that it could serve as a reference work and the basis for exploration for the kick-lover. I did try to start this potentially huge work, probably imperfectly, with a series of Books I chose to name the 'Kicks Series'. A global overview of Basic Kicks was presented in **'The Essential Book of Martial Arts Kicks'** (Tuttle), translated in several foreign languages. Its success lead me to follow with the important lower gates attacks in **'Low Kicks'**, and then **'Stop Kicks'** about preempting, jamming, impaling, obstructing and 'cutting' Kicks. As a sign of these MMA times, the series was naturally enriched by **'Ground Kicks'**. **'Stealth Kicks'** then endeavored to cover misdirection and dissimulation while kicking. Now comes this volume, **'Sacrifice Kicks'** about Flying and Suicide Kicks. And we hope that all this work will be built upon by others in the future. As mentioned and underlined many times, kicking proficiency requires a lot of serious drilling. I have therefore also published a work about the basic general drills that will help you reach higher levels of proficiency. As in all athletic endeavors, it is the basic drills that will build the strong foundation needed; and it is to those basic drills that the truly good athlete will come back for further progress again and again. **'Plyo-Flex Training for Explosive Martial Arts Kicks and Other Performance Sports'** does present those general, basic but so-important exercises that one should regularly practice for continuous improvement of kicking proficiency.

And now last, but certainly not least: it is important to underline that my strong views do not try in any way or form to denigrate the Punching Arts. My personal philosophy is that Martial arts are a whole with a world of possible emphasis. A complete Martial artist should be proficient in punching, kicking, moving, throwing, grappling, evading and more. But every Artist will have his own preferences and particular skills in his own way to look at the Martial Arts as a whole. ➜

...And here must I add the obvious: *there is no kicking mastery* without punching proficiency! Even for a dedicated kicker, punching will be needed for closing the gap, feinting, setting up a kick, following it up and much more... This will be made abundantly clear from most of the applications presented in this volume, just as it is clear from all my previous work.

It must be said that Punching is sometimes the best or the only answer in some situations. I have known and met some extraordinary Punching Artists using kicks only as feints or set-ups. On the other hand, great kickers like legendary *Bill 'Superfoot' Wallace* were extremely skilled punchers and working hard at it, as I personally experienced in a few seminars. Kick and Punch, Punch and Kick: well-rounded is the secret.

And this leads me naturally to my last point. I would not want my books and my views to be misunderstood as an appeal to always kick when fighting, and especially not as an appeal to always high-kick. The best kicker in the world should not execute a high Kick, *just because he can*. A Kick should only be delivered *because and when it is suitable* to a specific situation! Obvious maybe, but certainly worth reminding. In someone else's words:

Take things as they are. Punch when you have to punch. Kick when you have to kick.
~Bruce Lee

General Introduction: The 'Kicks' Series

This book is not a "How to" book for the beginner, but, hopefully, a reference work for the experienced Martial Artist. It presupposes the knowledge of stances, footwork, and concepts of centerline, guards, distance, evasions and more. It also expects from the reader a good technical level in his chosen Martial style, including kicking. As this work is building upon the *Essential* basic level towards more sophisticated kicking maneuvers, all *Essential Kicks* are considered mastered from the author's point of view. The reader is invited to consult previous work already mentioned above. This book is intended as a tool for self-exploration and research about kicking outside experienced Artists' specific style. Therefore, the description of the different kicks is very short and typical examples are only briefly explained. The author relies more on photos and illustrations to exemplify his point. Let the reader try it and adapt it to his liking and morphology. The author tends to prefer drawings over photographs to be able to underline salient points sometimes hidden in photos.

The experienced trainee will probably notice quickly that the basic background of the author is Japanese *Karate*. This cannot be avoided but was not deliberate. This book aspires to be as "style-less" as possible, as its purpose is to bridge across the different schools on the basis of common immutable principles. The author's philosophy is that Martial Arts are an interconnected whole, where styles are just interpretations of some principles and their adaptation to certain sets of strategies, rules, cultural constraints, or morphologies. It is one and same thing, although it may seem different from different angles. In the pictures and illustrations, the reader can see technical differences and adaptations from different styles. This is done on purpose to underscore the style-less philosophy of the treatise. Sometimes the foot of the standing leg is flat on the floor, as required in traditional Japanese styles, and sometimes the heel is up as in certain deliveries of Korean arts. It should be clear that the biomechanical principles are identical for trained artists and the small differences of emphasis are meaningless. It is more important for a trainee to adapt the technique to his morphology and preferences, once it is well mastered. This book definitely does not pretend to present an axiomatic way to kick! In the same vein, arms during kicking are sometimes close to the body in hermetic guard and sometimes loose and counterbalancing the kicking move. Hands can be open, or fists tight.

...Like in previous efforts, it has proved very difficult to name and organize the kicks into and within groups. The author has given the techniques descriptive names in English, whenever possible commonly used names. But the more complex, exotic and hybrid kicks have sometimes either several different appellations in use or none, while being difficult to describe. The names the author has chosen could certainly be disputed and improved upon by some. For the most basic kicks common to all styles, we have added the respective original foreign names. The author apologizes in advance to the purists of all styles: It is clear that the description of a technique cannot be in all details valid for all styles (For example, the basic Front Kick is taught differently in *Shotokan* karate than in *TaeKwonDo)*. The original foreign names in Japanese, Korean, Chinese or Portuguese are just there as an indication for further research by the reader. It should also be noted that some techniques have different names in different schools of the same Art! For the more complex or exotic kicks, we have purposely omitted original names. Only when a kick is especially typical of a certain style, did we mention it, as a tribute to the specific school. The author also apologizes for his arbitrary transcription of foreign names, as purists could dispute the way it was done.

The kicks presented in this volume are tagged "Advanced". This does not necessarily mean that they are more difficult to execute than the *Essential* basic kicks. On the contrary. Besides being a requisite of some form of classification, it mainly means that the principles behind the "basic" kicks should be first thoroughly mastered. A *Front Stop Kick* is relatively easy to perform and slightly different than a regular Front Kick. But for maximum power, it is important to follow the same principles of a basic Front Kick, with chambering, kicking through and chamber back. And the principles of the leg development stay the same for the more difficult Flying Front Kick. And even if a Low Front kick seems easy to perform, it will be done so under the same principles already mastered for maximum speed and power. A typical Feint Kick, the Roundhouse-chambered Front Kick is slightly tricky to master, but it is more a question of hip flexibility and acquaintance drilling: the principles behind the power of what is ultimately a Front Kick stay the same. Once the principles behind the basic Front Kick are mastered, all other "Advanced" kicks will be faster and more powerful. **This is all about mastering the basics and principles first**, and only later trying out variations in all kinds of situations, fancier or not. This is, by the way, true for any other physical activity. But because Advanced Kicks are more a variation on the theme of their underlying basic kicks, they will be presented in all their complexity by many variations in specific applications.

This volume will not detail *Essential* basic kicks. If needed for the clarity of the narrative, some of them will be very briefly illustrated as a reminder... ➡

This volume deals with *Jumping, Flying, Hopping and Suicide Kicks* only, as a variation of all six basic categories of Essential Kicks presented in previous work (Front, Side, Back, Roundhouse, Hook and Crescent Kicks). Further volumes are in preparation to present the complex Multiple kicks, the devastating Joint kicks and the no-nonsense Self-Defense Kicks.

Some Advanced Kicks have been omitted, as the author felt he had to draw the line somewhere. Again the decision was arbitrary, and could be considered as open for discussion. First have been omitted the whole range of nuances of a given kicks: As already mentioned, the same basic kicks are delivered in slightly different ways in all different styles and schools. The small differences come from the different emphasis of each style, and do not alter the basic principles. The author therefore described the kicks in the way his own experience dictates as best, and each reader can adapt it to his own personality. Many possible variations are presented for completeness in the applications though.

Flying Knee Strike

Secondly, hybrid kicks variations have been omitted, as the infinite number of intermediate possible deliveries in between two kicks would make this endeavor ridiculous. For example, many possible kicks as hybrids of Front and Roundhouse Kicks exist, each one with different levels of emphasis on the "front" side and the "roundhouse" side. In this specific book about Jumping Kicks of all types, it is even truer: there are a great number of deliveries possibilities to execute a Flying Front Kick, as the length and height of the jump is highly dependent on the circumstances and the reaction of the opponent.

Kicks combinations, and kick-punch combinations are infinite in numbers and will not be presented as such; *but hinted at in the Applications.* Knee strikes, although very effective and versatile, will not be presented; for the purpose of this work, they will not be considered as kicks.

The remaining **'Suicide' Kicks** which will be presented in this work, will be so, generally, in a set descriptive way: After a brief **General** introduction and the **Description** of the kick (mainly by illustrations), the main **Key Points** to remember for a good execution will be noted. Please remember that the book is intended for conversant martial artists. The relevant **Targets** to be kicked in most applications will be mentioned, although only general targets will be mentioned: The specific and precise vulnerable points are out of the scope of this volume. Examples of **Typical Applications** will then be detailed and illustrated. The typical application will generally be, unless irrelevant, a detailed use or set up of the given kick in a tournament-type situation. ➤

This will generally be a movements combination based on alternating different attack angles or/and levels (For example: hi-lo-hi, or/and outside/inside/outside), or the Progressive Indirect Attack principle as it is called by *Jeet Kune Do* artists. The tactical principle involved will not be detailed or presented systematically though, as it is beyond the scope of this volume. Of course, those applications will also usually be relevant to real life situation, and training work.

Whenever possible, **Specific Training** tips to improve the given kick will be detailed. The specific training section will be brief and will only deal with the very specific characteristics of the kick and the ways to perfect them; general kick training guidelines are outside the scope of this book. The training of a *Flying Kick* is generally also the drilling of the corresponding Essential basic kick, before the merging with a jump of some sort. Back to basics then! Last, and in order to widen the scope of applications, additional examples of the use of the kick will be presented, generally more suitable to a **Self-defense** or Mixed Martial Arts application.

And now the reader is asked to remember that the fact that this particular book (and the whole 'Kicks' Series) has cataloged a great number of kicks does not mean that he has to know and master them all. As already mentioned, a good Martial Artist must first master the basics of his chosen style by hard work on the *Essential* techniques. Only when he has done so, should he try advanced maneuvers and special techniques from other Arts. He should then drill new and unconventional techniques, and then try them in free fighting. A real Artist will then know how the choose only *a few* techniques that are suitable to his morphology, psychology and liking. These very few techniques will then have to be drilled for thousands and thousands of times until they become natural. During the fight, it the *body* that intuitively choses the best technique to be used. If you have to think about what to do, you have already lost! Practice makes perfect. Again, in other people'words:

I fear not the man who has practiced 10,000 kicks once, but I fear the man who has practiced one kick 10,000 times.
~ Bruce Lee

Train hard, fight easy
~Alexander Suvorov

So drill the Kicks and Applications as presented. Then adapt them to your physiology and psychology. Keep drilling and try them in free fighting. The follow-up presented are indicative only and intended to make you think. Try them before replacing by your own. And now, let us go to SACRIFICE KICKS...

Introduction to Sacrifice Kicks

We titled this book: 'Sacrifice Kicks' for a very good reason. We could have named it: Airborne Kicks, Flying Kicks or Jumping Kicks. But we choose the more general and meaningful term **Sacrifice**. It is meant in the spirit of 'Sutemi Waza' of Judo and old Jiu-Jitsu, meaning sacrificing your *balance* and your own *standing* posture in order to take down your opponent. The *Sacrifice Throws* of Judo and Jiu-Jitsu are extremely efficient and they should even be preferred if you are a good grappler and intend to take the fight to the floor.

For our kicking purposes, the 'sacrifice' means *giving up* on your standing posture and on the standing leg *anchoring* you to the ground, in order to succeed with an Airborne Kick and its special characteristics. Sacrifice Kicks can be further but loosely classified as either *Flying Kicks* or *Suicide Kicks*, both based on the same principles of sacrificing a stable upward position.

We shall present first the classic **Jumping Kicks** that can be used *high*, but also *long & low*. And we shall present also the more esoteric **Suicide Kicks**, more acrobatic and generally involving dropping or rolling to the floor. The classic Flying (or Jumping) Kicks are generally executed in a way that presupposes your <u>trying</u> to land back on your feet after kicking. On the other hand, the so-named Suicide Kicks are executed with the mindset of your finishing the technique on the floor. The difference is slightly semantic, but I think it certainly allows for a meaningful classification effort. I think that the distinction will be easier to understand with the actual description of the kicks. To paraphrase someone: difficult to define, but you know it when you see it.

Airborne kicks, whether executed flying high, jumping long, hopping, rolling or dropping low, have the physical disadvantage of lacking the anchor to the ground that will channel the reaction force from your 'action' on impact. The force of impact is therefore less focused and dissipates. The chambering-back, when possible and actually executed, is also much less effective. The contact at impact being longer because of the 'flying' momentum, the kick becomes more 'pushy' and less snappy. This is even truer for the *Straight* Flying Kicks.

But there are advantages too. A <u>*Sacrifice Straight Kick*</u> will have the advantage of the full momentum of your jump with the addition of your full body mass. When you kick normally grounded, you cannot put all your body mass in the game. And Energy is (Mass) x (the *square* of your velocity). Of course the square of velocity is huge, but using your full mass has also considerable weight in the formula. It should be clear to all. Of course, any *improvement* in your given speed will enjoy the square power advantage. But it will only be incremental: you will not be able to double your speed, unless you have been incredibly slow before. So Mass is good after all…

...Moreover, Sacrifice Kicks, especially of the flying type, have also a tremendous **psychological** impact: they are fully committed and extremely energetic. They are generally unexpected and they also carry a surprisingly powerful momentum. For example, they are great in a self-defense situation to break an encirclement.

The _Circular Sacrifice Kicks_ are different from the straight ones and they have their specific advantages. The momentum forward will only help closing the distance as the Circular Kick itself is executed on another plane. The name of the game for Circular Flying Kicks is speed, and speed only. They are _kick-through_ kicks which power comes from acceleration. And in that, they even have a serious advantage on regular standing Circular Kicks: being airborne, the Circular Flying Kicks are not hindered in their rotation by the standing foot on the floor! The pivot can be faster and looser.

In summary, the Kicks that we shall describe in this book are delivered while going off-balance or while going fully airborne. These kicks have advantages and disadvantages and have to be used accordingly, as the circumstances dictate. Some of the kicks, especially the high flying ones, are more suitable for some physiologies and body types; this is also a factor in drilling and using them. I must confess that I am personally not an assiduous user of high Flying Kicks: I tended to use them quite a lot in free-fighting when I was younger and weighing 150 pounds, but at the top of my sporting career at 210 pounds, I used only one or two, and very parsimoniously for the effect of surprise (The Offensive Front Kick to Flying Roundhouse combination, and the Flying Spin-back Outside Crescent Stop Kick).

I want to underline that I have the utmost respect for Martial Arts ripe with Flying and Suicide Kicks like _Tae Kwon Do_ and _Capoeira_ among others, -both Arts that I have had some training in. But my body type, my affinities and my preferences make this type of acrobatic kicks less attractive.

But I also want to underline that I am convinced that _students of all Arts should drill Sacrifice Kicks_, even if it is outside the scope of their schools or if it is physically difficult for them. First, every Martial Artist should understand the mechanics of an Airborne Kick for general kicking proficiency. Second, some will develop an affinity for some of those kick and gain a surprising and effective technique in their personal arsenal. Third, one should drill any technique that could be used against himself by a proficient Artist. And finally, those kicks can be very helpful if your loss of balance is accidental and not intended! And I want to remind the reader that a Jumping Kick does not necessarily mean high: it can mean **long and low**.

Success is where preparation and opportunity meet
~Bobby Unser

PART ONE

CLASSIC FLYING KICKS

FLYING KICKS- GENERAL

In Martial Arts, every time you graduate, move to another level, you do not forget everything you have done. You build on it, but it is always there
~Melody Beattie

1. INTRODUCTION

This section about **Flying Kicks** will present Kicks delivered airborne in such a way that the Artist **expects landing on his feet at the end of the execution**. These could be considered like 'half-suicide' techniques: one sacrifices his balance momentarily, but expects to recover it at the end of the maneuver. These are the classic Jumping Kicks as taught in most mainstream Martial Arts. These are basic Essential Kicks, but executed while jumping, hopping or scissoring the legs airborne. This distinction is made to differentiate the Flying Kicks from the *Suicide Kicks* presented in the second part of the book. (The Artist executing a Suicide Kick does not expect to land on his feet, but plans to crash on the ground after or while scoring with his kick)

Flying Kicks are probably the most spectacular Martial Arts kicks, and they are used as the most impressive in Martial Arts movies. They are not, though, the most important, effective or even practical kicks.
Flying Kicks do have certain advantages, and can be highly suitable for certain situations. But they are not for everyone: They are more suitable to certain morphologies, and, in any case, they require a lot of training to be efficient (See last section of this part one, about Plyometric Exercises). The delivery of such kicks is also fraught with dangers and disadvantages.

Marc - Typical Seventies haircut

But let us start on a positive note with the ***advantages*** of Flying (or Jumping) Kicks:

- The most important advantage of a Flying Kick is, in my opinion, the effect of **surprise**. Doing the unexpected will always give you an edge. The sudden delivery of a *straight* Flying Kick is always unsettling; therefore surprising. And *circular* Flying Kicks are usually very fast, and therefore the kick itself is hard to detect before impact and rather unexpected.
- *Straight* Flying Kicks, -like Front Flying Kicks or Side Flying Kicks-, do provide the **momentum** of the jump in the same line vector as the kick development. This does deliver a huge amount of energy with the kick, as the whole body mass is behind it. As power is a multiple of mass, you hit your opponent with the accelerating mass of the whole body, instead of the leg only.
- The jump, in a *straight* Flying Kick, also allows a **fast covering of distance**: There is no way a retreating opponent can run backwards faster than a forward jump. And those kicks are sometimes delivered after a few steps, or even after a run-up! You can therefore basically close the distance *while* kicking.
- A straight Flying Kick is a very effective way to **break out** of a ring of encircling opponents, because surprising, energetic and distance-covering.
- *Circular* Flying Kicks, like the Flying Roundhouse Kick or the Flying Spin-back Hook Kick, do lose a lot of the forward momentum advantages, but they compensate for this by being very powerful in their own way. The lack of hindrance of a foot on the floor liberates the body for a fuller and **faster** circular spin. The centrifugal force that can be gathered by a faster spin in the air, allows for much more power than with the corresponding regular "floor" kick. We need to remember that, in the equation for power, speed is more important by an order of magnitude (square), than mass!
- Finally, short "air time" Double Flying Kicks allow for **fast switching legs**: You are not hindered by the constraints of a leg on the floor to double-kick! An example of that are the fast Double Roundhouse Kicks, -one leg, then the other-, often seen in *Tae Kwon Do* tournaments.

This list of advantages is certainly not negligible. Fighters interested and well-suited for Jumping and Flying Kicks will easily be able to make use of those techniques. But every coin has two sides…

Unfortunately, the use of Flying Kicks has its clear **_disadvantages_** to keep in mind for a judicious use:

- Flying Kicks require a lot of energy to execute well, and therefore are **exhausting** and require stamina. This is also the reason why those kicks are more suitable to the small and light ectomorphic fighter than to the endomorphic tall and heavy fighter.
- Once you are in the air, it is extremely difficult to change position or movement: You are basically at the mercy of your opponent. From this point of view, they are in my eyes real "Sacrifice" Kicks, with a pinch of suicidal. They are of the 'Fire & Forget' type: **fully committed and no going back**.
- After delivering a Flying Kick, you must land in position and with perfect balance, in order to be able to seamlessly keep fighting. This is not easy at all, and you are especially **vulnerable while landing** and recovering your balance. The classic counter against a Flying Kick is to attack the airborne or landing legs with a sweep or a low kick, as illustrated.

This leg sweep against a jumping kick will cause a very nasty fall

With all this being said, we must conclude that Flying Kicks are an important part of the kicker's arsenal. But, as already mentioned, they require a lot of stamina and proficiency, obtained only by long and thorough training. I have seen the most spectacular flying kicks used successfully in tournament fights, but always used parsimoniously as an *unexpected* surprise move by proficient fighters.

A further important point to emphasize is that a Flying Kick **needs not to be high to be efficient**. Jumping can be *long* instead of high, in order to allow to cover more *distance*. And it should be added that the foot of the leg that is not delivering the kick needs not be cocked high for aesthetics as often done. In fact, the closer the foot to the ground, the better for a quick recovery when landing! This distinction is clearly made in *Shotokan Karate*, where **_Tobikonde_** is a high Flying Kick, and **_Surikonde_** is a low & long forward-jumping kick. Both are versions of the same kick executed differently for different purposes. And of course, all variations in between both versions are valid. Just remember that a Flying Kick needs not to be aesthetically pleasing, but needs to be efficient as per the situation. Unless, of course, you are an actor in a Martial Arts movie!

*Flying Side Kick – **Tobikonde** (Rui Monteiro)*

*Flying Side Kick – **Surikonde** (Yannick Pierrard)*

And now a last word about **landing**. As already mentioned, landing in total control and balance is generally key to a successful fight. And classical Flying Kicks are executed as landing kicks: you expect and train for landing on your feet in fully focused guard (*Zanshin*). This is the definition we have given in this book for Flying Kicks, in order to differentiate them from Suicide Kicks. But it is not always easy! It must be mentioned that some styles encourage ground-fighting and the more acrobatic landings that we have here associated with Suicide Kicks. Hard training and proficiency in those exotic fighting arts allow for more flexibility in landing, but this becomes very style-specific. It is important to investigate though, as *the perfect landing is more the ideal exception than the rule*. It is particularly important with Double Flying Kicks for example: after hitting your opponents with both feet at the same time, in the air, it will be difficult to land squarely on your feet in perfect balance!

Styles like Japanese *Ninjitsu* will have you land and roll back in perfect *Ukemis* (fall breaks) and disappear. Some Southern Chinese styles relish fighting from the ground, so landing is no problem. *Capoeristas* fight always close to the ground, using the limbs and head as support in variable combinations. The point I am trying to make at this juncture is that, even if you fall after your Flying Kick, life is far from over and you can keep fighting. It is important, when jump-kicking, to be familiar with ground movement and, at least, with some ground -fighting basics. The reader is invited to refer, amongst others, to our previous book about 'Ground Kicks' which details ground movement and standing back up techniques. Ground Kicks are also the natural complement to bad landings and should be studied and drilled seriously... Just in case...

Twin-legs Flying kick : Beware of the landing!
(Dotan De Bremaeker)

2. JUMPING METHODS

There are basically **three jumping methods** for the delivery of Flying Kicks: 'Kicking leg leaves the floor last', 'Kicking leg leaves the floor first' and 'Both legs leave the floor simultaneously'. (Note: A fourth crude method would be running to gather momentum for the jump)

1.   *Jumping Method 1*: 'Kicking leg leaves the floor last'.
Raise one leg, front or rear, as if stepping onto an invisible step. Then use the other leg to jump up and kick. See Photos and illustrations below. There is a kind of "scissoring" of the legs in the air, when the kicking leg goes up and the other leg goes back down.

Lift one leg, jump up and kick with the other

Scissor in the air

2.   *Jumping Method 2*: 'Kicking leg leaves the floor first'.
Raise the kicking leg towards chambered position, and then jump off the other leg. See Photos and illustration. This is basically a big or a high "hopping" step, as in the basic Hopping version of the corresponding *Essential* Kick.

Basically a big hop

Side Kick: Lift the kicking leg and then jump

3.   *Jumping Method 3*: 'Both legs leave the floor simultaneously'.
Jump from both feet, and then kick when airborne. See photos and drawings at the top of next page.

➡

Jump high from both feet, then kick

Simple: Jump up and Kick!

3. FURTHER CLASSIFICATIONS

Flying Kicks can still be classified and described in other ways. Of course, as always, there are variations and sub-categories, but we will present them specifically and ad hoc. We will limit ourselves to the most used and most logical variations, as the number of possibilities is very high. Basically every kick can be delivered in a *combination* of all the following options:

a.   *Kick with Front leg or Rear leg.*

Front-leg *Flying Side Kick, hopping-style*

Rear-leg *Flying Side Kick*

It should further be noted that there are many different ways to execute a front-leg kick (or a rear-leg one for that matter). The Figures below show two very different <u>Front-Leg</u> Flying Front Kicks: one "*hopping*", and the other "*scissor-style*".

Front-leg Flying Front Kick, hopping-style

Front-leg Flying Front Kick, Scissor-style

b.   Execute a High jump or a Long hop

High-jump Flying Front Kick
(**Tobikonde Mae Tobi Geri**)

Low but long hop-Flying Front
Kick (**Surikonde Mae Tobi Geri**)

c.   Have the Kicking leg leave the floor first, last or simultaneously, as previously detailed in the *Jumping Methods* section.

d.   Do a full leg switch or a simpler hopping movement, when airborne.

Leg switch is an airborne Scissor. A high hopping maneuver means one leg "replaces and pushes" the other forward.

Full scissoring leg-switch while airborne

High hopping front-leg Flying Front Kick

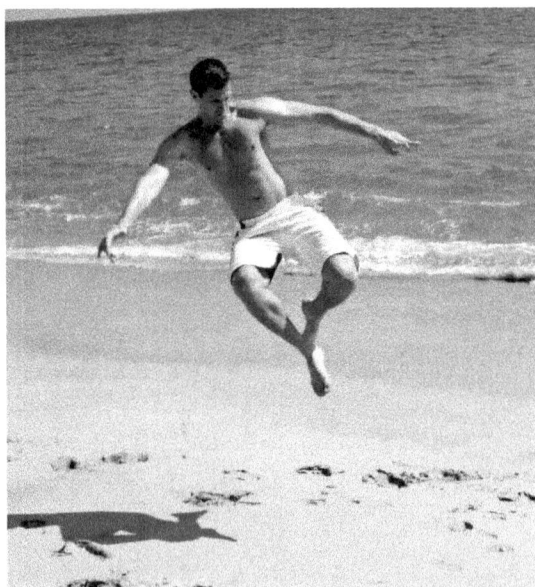

Clear airborne hopping: just like a regular (non-flying) front-leg kick, but simply higher

e. **_Keep the non-kicking leg coiled or straight._**

A direct comparison is presented in the Illustrations.

Coiled or straight non-kicking leg:
The difference is mainly aesthetic

The more spectacular coiled-leg version of the
Flying Front Kick

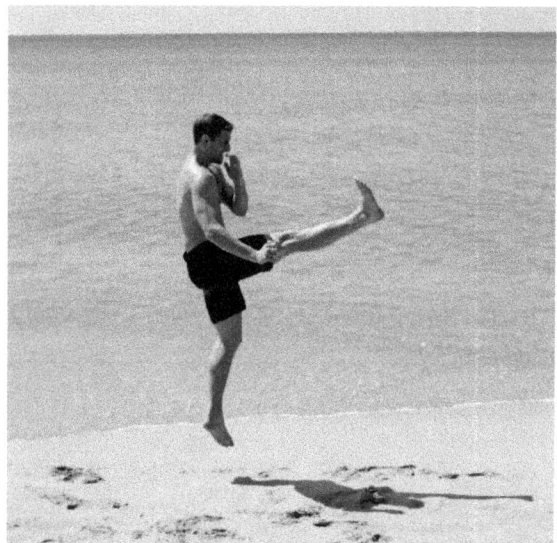

The straight non-kicking leg does not make the
Flying Kick less effective

And Now, on to the Classic Flying Kicks...

You can't put a limit on anything. The more you dream, the farther you get.
~Michael Phelps

THE KICKS

1. THE FLYING FRONT KICK

Mae Tobi Geri (Karatedo), Du Bal Dang Sang (TaeKwonDo), Fey Tshe (Kung Fu), Phi Tieu Cuoc (Viet VoDao), Grad Dod Teep (Muay Thai), Tobi Geri Taihen (Ninjitsu), Bençao pulada/ Ponteira pulada (Capoeira)

General

The Flying Front Kick is probably the easiest Flying Kick to master, and it is where the beginner should start. It is a very effective kick, especially in its "jumping-forward" version. And it is a relatively safe kick to deliver because, during delivery, there is uninterrupted eye contact and there is always a limb between you and your opponent. It is interesting to note that this is the only "Flying" Kick appearing in some way in old traditional Japanese forms, and still very sparingly. Again, there is no doubt that this is the first Flying Kick that the beginner should work on and strive to master, in all possible variations as described in the Introduction.

Description

The reader is invited to continuously refer to the introduction as for all the different ways to deliver a Flying Kick. We will present here only some of those different ways, in their practical form and in no particular order.

Jump off both feet

The first Illustrations present a *"both-feet-leave-the-ground-simultaneously"* type of delivery, using the rear leg for the kick. You basically jump up from both feet and deliver in the air a regular rear-leg front kick; thus landing in opposite position. This is a kick for height, not distance.

The next examples, at the top of next page, will present *"kicking-foot-leaves-ground-last"* -types of delivery, both for a front-leg Kick.

➡️

The first of those Kicks presents the classic "*scissor-in-the air*" delivery, which is a great help for achieving height or distance: You lift the rear knee forward **as if you were stepping on an *invisible* high step to help propel you upwards**. This mindset helps the explosiveness of your up and forward momentum. While using this invisible step to propel yourself up, you lift off the kicking leg (Formerly front leg) and lift the knee high in coiled position, so replacing the other knee in a scissor-like movement. From this coiled position you deliver the Front Kick before landing on the other leg first. Note that the non-kicking leg can immediately be re-extended towards the floor, or stay bent close to your groin for as long as possible (Note: this is true for most flying kicks).

Step onto invisible prop and scissor up

The second example shows a more 'economic' version of this kick, faster than the previous delivery, but shorter in achievable range. In fact, this is basically an *Essential* front-leg **Hopping** Kick, where the rear leg replaces the kicking front one. Should you aim for distance, against a retreating opponent for example, it is then just a long hopping front-leg Front Kick, maybe slightly higher for longer reach. If you are also trying to achieve some height, then it is useful to imagine again a stepping stone to help you go up. But this time the imaginary step is just behind your front leg, and your rear foot comes forward higher than for a hop, to push the front leg forward and up (but from a higher position). This kick could be considered an abbreviated version of the previous one where you do not cross forward in your step. Or, alternatively, it could be considered a supersized version of the *Essential* classic Hopping front-leg Front Kick.

A high front-leg Hopping Kick

Key points

- The Kick itself must be delivered just as a regular basic 'floor' Front Kick; with hip push, full chamber and full chamber-back.
- Especially with Flying Kicks, it is important that the recoil be full and immediate after impact.
- Always aim to land in a low strong position, focused, ready and with your guard up.

Targets

All the upper body is a target. Should you be able to jump high, the head becomes an easier target than for a grounded Front Kick. Remember also that Flying Kicks can be delivered *low and long*, and therefore used very successfully for lower belly and groin kicks! Some of the Illustrative Photos at the end of the section illustrate a *high* Flying Front Kick targeting the *lower* ribs.

Typical Applications

The Figures below will show a third possible delivery type, less practical for a simple straightforward attack, but very suitable as a more sophisticated feint move. The kicking foot leaves the ground first, but pauses to break the rhythm. You lift your rear knee in a classic Front Kick chamber, ideally after delivering a few of those basic floored Front Kicks to get your opponent used to them. You so cause him to block or protect his lower belly, and then jump forward and up while delivering your real (flying) Front Kick towards his sternum. In doing so, you are also getting high and close while smothering his arms and defense, so that you can deliver one, or even two punches to his exposed face as well.

Feint, Pause, Jump up

Specific Training

- To help your form, deliver the kick in technically-perfect form, while getting help to stay airborne a little bit longer: using a dancing ramp or being helped by a partner (See Illustrations at the top of next page). You could also use a trampoline or jumping into a pool!
- Use a high "step", -stool or box-, to get the feeling of the '*invisible step*' jumping method. It will also help you staying airborne for technical excellence. It is also a strength-bolstering exercise (Illustrated at the top of next page).

Use help to stay airborne longer for better form

Use a box to jump up higher

- Train for strength, explosive power and endurance by jumping from crouched position as high as possible while hitting your own chest with your knees or reaching with the knees outside your shoulders (See Photos). This is of course relevant training for all jumping kicks.

Jumping exercise

- Repeat the jumping exercise, but this time, deliver the Flying Front Kick from the low crouched position, as illustrated.

Drill the Flying Front Kick by exploding up from the kneeling position

- You must be able to control your kick for distance and/ or height, and use it only when and where needed. Therefore heavy bag training is very important: Mark different heights on the bag and different starting distances on the floor. Kick exactly where and from where you have decided. Repeat while varying.

Precision training: Learn to deliver the kick from any distance and to any height required

Self defense

As a straightforward kick, the Flying Front Kick is a great kick for self-defense. It has great power and forward momentum for overpowering and stunning an opponent (or to break an encirclement). Remember that most of the time, **simple and straight is the best policy: if confronted, kick early and decisively.** This said, we will present the kick here in a more complex combination though, and always remember that you can kick either *long* (a retreating assailant) or *high* (if the assailant stays in place).

➡️

...The Figures below show a great and simple combination attack starting with the delivery of an *Essential* floored rear-leg Front Kick. As the opponent blocks the kick, you chamber back and lower the leg back where it came from. **But you let it *rebound* on the floor** to let the knee come back up forward again. This looks like a chamber of the same Front Kick which should entice the same blocking pattern from your opponent. But the chamber is in fact an "*invisible step-up*" preparation for a Flying Front Kick from the other leg.

Feint regular Front Kick; then deliver 'stepping' Flying Front Kick with the other leg

Illustrative Photos

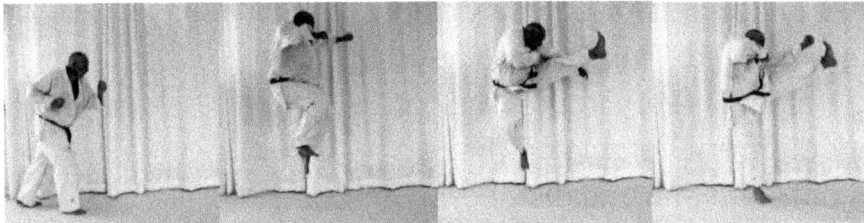

R. Monteiro – Flying Front Kick, extended leg

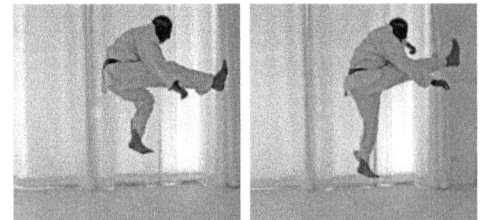

*A "**Both-feet-leave-the-ground-simultaneously**" Rear-leg Flying Front Kick*

Non-Kicking leg can be straight or bent

Keeping the non-kicking leg extended makes for a safer landing and a more powerful kick, without losing the aggressiveness and momentum of the Flying Kick

*Flying Front Kick to the **lower ribs**: A high jump for a low target, powerful and unexpected*

Front Flying Kick: Kicking leg leaves floor first

Front Flying Kick: Kicking leg leaves floor last

Most people never run far enough on their first wind to find out they've got a second.
~William James

2. The Double Flying Front Kick Combination

Nidan Geri (Karatedo)

General

This is, in the author's opinion, one of the most practical of all Flying Kicks: easy to perform, powerful, answering many realistic combat situations, good for competitive and real-life environment, and still somewhat sophisticated as a Double Kick. No wonder that it is one of the few Flying Kicks encountered in authentic traditional Karate forms (*Gankaku Kata* of the *Shotokan-ryu* style, for example).

This technique is basically a Flying Front Kick, but instead of the starting "*invisible step*" maneuver, comes another Flying or Hopping Front Kick. This Flying Double Kick is in fact a Flying Front Kick evolving through an "*airborne scissor*" into a second Flying Front Kick with the **other** leg (whence the name "combination").
We could have classified this kick as a Double Kick or a Feint Kick, and then presented it in other books. But it is an important Flying Kick taught separately, on its own advantages, as a basic kick in many schools. So here it is. In some variations, the first Kick is not a full Flying Kick: it can be a simple regular basic Front Kick or Hopping Front Kick. It does not change anything and the general idea or state-of-mind are the same. The seasoned martial artist will easily adapt the delivery to the situation, to his own preferences and to his affinities.

It becomes now unnecessary to remind the reader that, like for all Flying Kicks, the Double Flying Front Kick Combination can be executed high or long, and both variants should be practiced thoroughly. The long version is extremely useful against a retreating opponent, and it usually allows for catching up and scoring. This is an important kick! See the Illustrative Photos at the end of the section.

Excerpt of Gankaku no Kata of the Shotokan-ryu

Description

We will describe the two most practical delivery versions for this kick.
The first Figures below show the preferred powerful delivery: both feet leave the
ground *simultaneously* in a jump during which you
deliver an **airborne** rear-leg Front Kick. As soon as this
kick connects, you retract the kicking leg and lift the
other airborne knee into chamber position to deliver the
second Front Kick (with the other leg). You land in the
same position you started, having kicked with both legs.
Now, the illustrations below show a milder delivery, less
powerful but also less telegraphing. In this option, the
first kick is delivered in the "kicking-leg-leaves-the-ground-first"-style. Basically, the

Jump off both feet and double-kick

first Front Kick is more of an
Essential **Hopping** Front Kick,
but you do not wait to land
before you start the second
Front Kick with the other leg.
This is the preferred "long
kick" (*Surikonde*) version. It is
fast and surprising.

Hopping Front Kick and scissoring airborne into the capping Flying Front Kick

Key points

- This is a *Double* Kick and both kicks must be fully delivered: the first kick is not a feint but a kick!
- Keep your guard up, especially when landing.

Targets

Like for the regular Flying Front Kick, all targets are relevant from the groin up. Being a Double Kick, it is tactically advantageous to try to kick at different levels, for example: first kick to the lower belly and second kick to the face. This is just an example, and all permutations should be experimented with.

Typical Applications

The Illustrations below show the applied variation in which the first kick is basically a regular *on-the-ground* Front Kick, although given with extra forward momentum. This is a typical "long" combination, destined to overpower a *retreating* opponent: the kicks are delivered while jumping **forward** and **close to the floor**. In the example, you open with a classic high jab/high cross/body rear-leg Front Kick combination attack. You are, by doing so, forcing your opponent to block and retreat. Your committed Front Kick is a *long* extended kick with a lot of momentum and hip forward thrust. When it recoils, you jump forward off the standing leg which becomes the kicking leg. The second kick is definitely a Flying Kick and it can target the lower abdomen if your opponent has over-blocked the first kick, or the face if the opponent's trunk is still well guarded. But please note that this kind of kick is *powerful* enough to penetrate the guard itself, making the guarding hands of the opponent a non-issue. And remember also that nobody can run backwards as fast as you can run and jump forward! All these make this simple but fantastic combination an important to drill.

A typical Blitz against a retreating opponent

The following drawings show an exotic variation often found in Northern styles of *Kung Fu*. In this case, the first *grounded* Kick hits the opponent's elbow, whether he is in guard or whether he is developing a punch. The second kick, -the concluding Flying Front Kick-, uses the diversion to aim with great momentum for the upper body, the face or the throat. This is, of course, a **high and short-range** version of the kick; it is not 'Surikonde' material. Which shows how versatile these techniques are...

Pop the front arm up as a diversion and scissor in a Flying Front Kick

Specific training

- Work on your jumps, just like for the regular Flying Front Kick already presented.
- Practice on the heavy bag but **mark** the distances from the bag and **mark** the different target levels on the bag (Illustrated). When training for distance control on a *long* kick, deliver the first kick in the air and then hit the bag with the second kick. When training for *height*, let both kicks hit the bag. Always try to hit the bag at the specifically marked places.

Master distance and height

Self defense

This is now a great *Triple* Kick combination, especially suitable when the situation warrants you to show very aggressive behavior. The drawings show how you are being clearly threatened by an assailant, in this case holding a stick. As he starts to move, or just gathers confidence to attack, you take preventive offensive action with a combined *simultaneous* rear-leg Front Kick to the belly and a high Reverse Punch to the face. This maneuver will make sure his senses are overwhelmed and he will not be able to complete an effective stick strike. You recoil your kicking leg and let it *rebound* back from its starting position to become the first front kick of your Double Flying Front Kick Combination. Your first kick will probably condition him to *try* to block the second kick <u>down</u>, opening him <u>up</u> for the third Flying Kick, <u>up</u>. The forward momentum of the whole combination will hinder any counterattack and keep you off the list of easy victims.

An overwhelming Blitz as a preemptive attack

Illustrative Photos

The Double Flying Front Kick combination is great to close the distance on a retreating opponent; it exemplifies that a flying kick needs not be high but is best sometimes long and low

3. THE DOUBLE FLYING FRONT KICK

Il Ja Tshagi (Tae Kwon Do)

General

This is quite an acrobatic kick and, in my opinion, not a very practical one. You jump up from both feet to simultaneously front-kick in the air **with both legs**. It is still a realistic maneuver that I have seen delivered impressively by *Ninjitsu* Artists, for example from close up after a double eardrum palm strike. And I think this exemplifies the way this kick is to be used: as a surprising and devious technique, with also some psychological impact. It is especially suitable for styles accustomed to falling and rolling on the floor. In any case, it is a great technique to train with for the general improvement of Flying Kicks, for the acquisition of endurance and for the development of power explosiveness.

The acrobatic Double Flying Front Kick. Beware of the landing!

Description

There are two basic ways to deliver the kick: with the legs parallel and **inside** the arms, or with the legs apart **outside** the arms (kicking two opponents simultaneously). Both ways are compared in the Illustrations below. To kick, you simply jump off both feet simultaneously and front-kick with both legs. You then try to reception yourself on both legs in a low stable position, guard up. Alternatively, you can let yourself fall to the floor and roll away. This technique obviously requires serious drilling.

Double Flying Front Kick, legs inside the arms

Double Flying Front Kick, legs outside the arms

Compared top views of both versions of the Double Flying Front Kick: Legs-together or Split

The kick can also be delivered as a "*running*" kick, after a few steps to gain momentum; the feet do not leave the ground exactly simultaneously, but the general feeling is the same (See Photos at the top of next page). Note that both kicks do not have necessarily to connect at the same level, as illustrated in the first application of the coming section.

➡️

If possible, run into the Double Flying Kick

Key points

- The kicks are still full-fledged kicks to be delivered in the manner of the traditional Front Kick: chamber, kick, recoil.
- If you choose to land on your feet, and succeed: keep your guard up.

Typical Application

The drawings below illustrate an example of the Kick delivered at close quarters, with both feet connecting **at slightly different levels**. The application presented is tactically one of the better uses of the kick, as you jump-kick from your opponent's "blind" outside, after his Reverse Punch attack. In the example, you also use his own body to push yourself into the jump, by catching his punching wrist first and then his shoulder. One foot can kick the solar plexus, while the other attacks the lower ribs *from the outside.*

Use the opponent to "pull" yourself up into the jumping kick. Deliver from the opponent's blind side

Specific training

- Practicing this kick is in itself a great conditioning exercise.
- Drill the kick from the knee-bent position, as illustrated. A variation of this exercise calls for sitting on your heels in traditional posture (Zeiza), then rolling back on your toes to crouched knee-bent position, and then jump up (See Illustrations).
- Practice on the heavy-bag from a marked distance. Always aim for the marks on the bag. Train for both high kicks at head level, and for more effective low kicks to the belly.

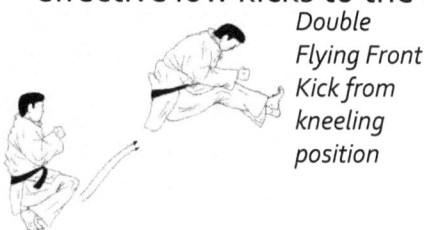

Double Flying Front Kick from kneeling position

Same drill starting from sitting on your heels

Self defense

The Illustrations show an example of a "running" version of the Kick. You are confronted by an assailant threatening to attack you and expecting you to flee. Do the unexpected and run towards him for maximum momentum into the Double Flying Kick. Not only will he be surprised and overwhelmed, but he will also have had misjudged distance for attack or counter. You have made an assertive preemptive strike and projected that you are not a victim.

Surprise your assailant by rushing him

Illustrative Photos

Twin Flying Front Kick to the groin area

Not a very practical kick but a spectacular one and a great jumping drill

There is no substitute to jumping drills for Flying Kicks progress

4. THE FLYING FRONT ANGULAR KICK

General

This is the **flying** version of the Essential 'Instep Angular Kick' or 'Lotus Kick'. This is not a very powerful kick but it is very fast and surprising. And it should be noted that the upward momentum of the flying version gives the kick some extra power, although it will still usually require a follow-up. All in all, the *Flying Lotus Kick* is quite easy to master and useful when mastered.

Description

As it is a 'speed' kick, it will usually be delivered with the **partial step-up** for take-off: the rear leg comes forward but will not complete the full step. The Illustrations show how the rear leg comes approximately to front leg level, pushing it up while (as if) stepping on an invisible step. You then scissor up into a classic *Essential Instep Angular Kick* (a hybrid Front Kick and Outside Crescent Kick) to hit your opponent's head upwards and from the side.

This kick delivery can go all the way from the slightly Hopping Instep Angular Kick, to the extreme variation of a full high Flying Kick. The principles stay the same. All variations are relevant, though the one presented is, in the author's opinion, the most practical.

Hop up into airborne Front-leg Lotus Kick

Key points

- You are not jumping up and forward only, but also *slightly to your inside*. It allows for the kick to be free to go up unhindered and to gather speed before impact.
- Keep your guard up at all times; this is a close-up Kick.

Targets

Mostly the head. Eventually the arms.

Typical Application

The Illustrations below show a pressure combination to be used on a blocking opponent: You keep up unrelenting pressure forward until you score! You keep attacking him with no hiatus, *but always at mid-level*, to force him to block and retreat. In the example are presented a body Jab, a rear-leg Front Kick, another body Jab, all in series. If possible, try to grab his arm after the last Jab, just for a second, as an attention diverter. You then jump forward (and to your in-side) into your intended *high* Flying Front Angular Kick. Aim for the ear.

Keep the pressure forward and at mid-level until you can squeeze in the Flying Lotus Kick

Specific training

- Practice the regular **grounded** *Instep Angular Kick*.
- This is a kick that must be practiced with a moving partner holding a striking pad at head level (As illustrated in the **Description**).

Self defense

The Figures *at the top of next page* show another example in which you confront an assailant by going forward, instead of retreating as he expects. When your opponent comes menacingly forward, you unexpectedly jump forward into the kick, up and slightly obliquely over the center-line. The Jumping Kick keeps you relatively safe from his attacks, even should he attempt a Front Kick. Your going forward confounds his expectations and his range expectations. We have presented here, for the sake of completeness, the variation in which the rear foot step-up is done *behind* the front leg. All principles apply as well. Please note that, in a self-defense situation with hard shoes on, the kicking foot could be turned outward to allow for connecting with the tip of the shoe, in the manner of an Essential '*Outward-tilted Front Kick*'.

➤

Do not retreat! Jump forward and out of the centerline, and kick

Illustrative Photos

The classic grounded Lotus Kick: becoming **Outside Crescent** *from* **Front** *chamber position*

The classic **Outward-tilted Front Kick,** *slightly curving out during extension*

5. THE FLYING SIDE KICK

Yoko Tobi Geri (Karatedo), Dtuiyu Yup Chagi (TaeKwonDo), Thang Thien Hoanh Sat Cuoc/ Phi Bang Sat Cuoc (Viet Vo Dao), Chapa Pulada (Capoeira)

General

The Flying Side Kick is probably the most popularized of all Flying Kick, seen in movies and magazines as the archetype of the spectacular Oriental Arts Flying Kicks. Being a straight kick just like the Flying Front Kick, it is a very powerful kick delivered in the same direction as the jumping momentum. It has even advantages over the Flying Front Kick: the 'side' hip thrust and also more body protection during the execution.

The Flying Side Kick can be delivered in a wide range of ways. Of course, we have the 3 classic **jump** possibilities, but each version can also be delivered with the *front* leg or with the *rear* leg (requiring a stepping twist, either airborne or on the ground). The Kick can also be delivered jumping *forward* (retreating opponent or breaking out of a ring of assailants), jumping *in place* (blocking/countering opponent), jumping *back* (timing Stop Kick) or directly to your side (See the first Figure of the *Description* section). You usually land in a strong stance, but further options for all types would be to let yourself fall low, or to roll to switch to ground-fighting. Try to practice as many of those permutations as possible, in order to become versatile and to be able to side-fly-kick instinctively.

It is also important to mention that the Flying Side Kick is a **Stop Kick** par excellence, mainly because the body is somewhat protected during the chambering as illustrated in some of the *Illustrative Photos* further in the text.

Description

We will describe here **three** examples of the three different main *jumping styles*:

The **first** set of illustrations shows a *"both-feet-leave-the-ground-simultaneously"* delivery type, with the Side Kick is delivered directly sideways. It is a good way to start drilling.

➡

Flying Side kick directly to your side; both feet leave the ground simultaneously

The **second** set, photos this time, show a "*kicking-leg-leaves-ground-first*"-delivery type. This is a rear-leg kick forward, with an airborne hip twist, after the kicking leg has used the invisible step to propel the body up and forward.

The rear leg leaves the ground first, but will be the kicking leg; strong forward momentum is needed

The **third** set, also photographic, shows finally a "*kicking-leg-leaves-ground-last*" delivery type, in a *front-leg* kick application. This is basically a "supersized" Essential Hopping front-leg Side Kick, with the rear leg coming forward to the invisible step.

An exaggerated Hopping Side Kick becomes a Flying Kick

Key points

- The Flying Side Kick is a **Side Kick first**, to be executed by all the basic rules: chambering, thrusting the hips at impact and recoil!
- Keep the guard up when landing.
- Try to delay the kicking for as long as possible, and kick just before starting to land.

Targets

From groin up to the head, everything is a target, as it is an extremely *powerful* kick. There is even a variation of the kick common from Vietnamese arts, where you jump *high* to kick *down* at knee level. It will be presented separately further in the text.

Typical application

The example illustrated below shows a typical applied use in a classic "**False Retreat**" tactic. When your opponent steps forward for a front-leg Side or Hook Kick, you retreat with your front leg *while evading out of the center-line*. But this is only to *rebound* back in a forward jump from both feet. Your jump will turn into a Flying Side Stop Kick to the head. This tactical maneuver allows you to come onto him from outwards and also from above his kicking leg. Although the illustrated jump is a *"both-legs"* version, it could also be of the *"kicking-leg-leaves-floor-first"* type.

Retreat and evade out, then rebound unexpectedly forward into a Flying Side Kick through his attack

Specific training

- This is a power kick that needs to be practiced on the heavy bag, from different distances. Range control is of the utmost importance. Also always mark the bag to force yourself to be precise in the delivery of the kick (As illustrated).

Drill the heavy bag with intended precision

- Practice the kick in its **3** 'mindset' variations: jumping forward, jumping in place (stop-kick) and jumping backward (block-kick). The drawings are self-explanatory.
- As illustrated at the top of next page, drill the correct technical form by remaining airborne longer, helped by a dancing rail or hold up by a partner.
- Use a trampoline for a better feel of the way the kick is to be delivered airborne. It is both fun and a good drill.
- You should also drill with a heavily protected and moving partner for more realism. See Photo at the top of next page.

Yoko Tobi Geri *on the heavy bag*

Become versatile; kick while jumping forwards, in place and backwards

Use help to practice the correct airborne form

A thick body shield will allow drilling at full power against a partner

Self defense

As already mentioned, _Straight_ Flying Kicks, when used as **simple attacks,** are very useful in self-defense because they are very powerful and momentum-driven kicks. They are overpowering, surprising, aggressive and allow breaking through encirclement for example. There is no need for further presentation of the use of a simple single Flying Side Kick.

We will then show here a more sophisticated use of the kick: a surprising technique that makes use of a **low crouched position** from which a jump is natural. The Illustrations show how you step forward _but to the outside_ of your assailant while jabbing. Your jab is a feint turning seamlessly into a _low_ punch towards your assailant's groin, while you lower yourself by simply bending the knees. From this coiled position, you jump up (both feet) and deliver a front-leg Flying Side Kick to his head from his out-side. This is also a basic and effective _hi/lo/hi_ combination.

Illustrative Photos

Long and low Flying Side Kick
(**Surikonde**) by Ziv Faige

You are relatively protected during the jump and chambering of the Flying Side Kick; in this case "both-feet-leave-floor-simultaneously

'In-place' stop-version of the kick: stop the opponent's front kick in the bud, before it can develop

...or alternatively jump over his developing kick to deliver yours!

A timed and angling Flying Side Kick by Rui Monteiro

Flying Side Kick, 'kicking-leg-leaves-the floor-first'

6. THE FLYING SPIN-BACK SIDE KICK

General

The Spin-back Flying Side Kick is very much like its *Essential* grounded counterpart, the *Spin-back Side Kick* (See in the **Illustrative Photos** section below): its difficulty lies in the *combination of a <u>circular</u> Spin-back movement and a <u>straight</u> kick finish*. The kick is less powerful than the basic straight Flying Side Kick, as there is much less momentum forward towards the target. But there is, of course, the additional effect of surprise and the added power from the centrifugal force of the airborne Spin-back. Like all Spinning Flying Kicks, this kick requires a lot of specific training. Like all Spinning Kicks, it bears the inherent danger of losing eye contact with the opponent. But, like all Spinning Flying Kicks though, this kick has the advantage, over its grounded counterpart, of a faster and more powerful delivery because it is unhindered by the standing leg.
I must add that, of all the Spin-back Flying Kicks, I think this one is the most practical and most effective for most fighters. It is also, in my opinion, the Spin-back Flying Kick most suitable as a Stop Kick, because of its powerful straight finish.

Description

The first set of Figures below shows the basic delivery, which is also the best way to start practicing the kick: you spin-back *in place*, just like for a regular grounded Spin-back Side Kick. And, *while* executing the spinning movement, you jump up, -the kicking foot leaving usually the floor first (although some people like a jump very close to the "both-feet-simultaneously" type). You then deliver the kick airborne, just like a grounded straight Side Kick, *just as you get in line* and the spinning move winds naturally down.

The basic Spin-back Flying Side Kick

→

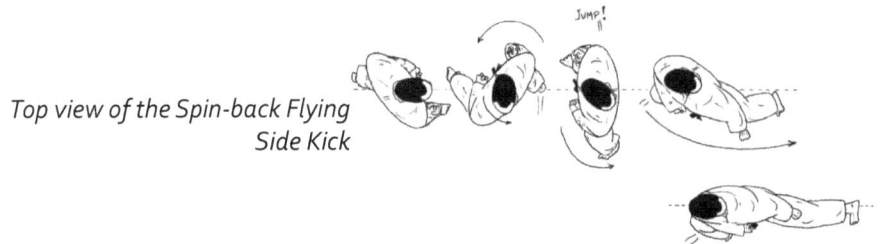

Top view of the Spin-back Flying Side Kick

Once you have mastered this *static* version of the kick, it is important to practice its natural flow when it is following a forward step or a backward step. The transition needs to be seamless and the way the step is done is in itself a subtle preparation for the Jumping Kick. Achieving this transition well requires work and intensive drilling.

The second set of Illustrations shows the delivery of the kick after a **forward** step: This is the closest thing to a full forward-momentum kick. You step forward and start spinning as soon as your foot touches the ground. Of course you step in a way that prepares your spin-back.

The third set shows in turn the kick delivered after a **backward** step: This is usually a "false retreat" tactic for a very powerful Stop Kick. Again, the backward step is already part of the spin-back!

Step forward while preparing the spin-back

The step back blends into the spin-back and then comes the Flying Stop Kick

Key points

- The energy in the spin-back is just enough to bring you in line for the straight Side Kick. If you spin too much, the Side Kick will fly obliquely and miss its target.
- Try to deliver the actual Side Kick at the last possible moment, before starting down towards landing.
- Keep your guard up when landing: remember that you have turned your back to the opponent.
- Full chamber and full recoil are of key importance; do not make this a 'pushing' kick.

Targets

From knee to head. The kick is powerful enough for body hits like sternum and lower abdomen attacks. It can even be used for devastating hip and knee joints attacks (See the **Illustrative Photos** section further down)

Typical application

The following Illustrations show what, in my mind, is the most suitable application of this Kick: the *"False Retreat" Spin-back stop-kicking* version. In the example, you have noticed that your opponent is fond of the typical Reverse Punch/rear-leg Roundhouse Kick offensive opening. As he launches another one of those, you step back into spin-back mode, just to jump back forward into the Kick. The Spin-back Flying Side Stop Kick will catch him *on the inside* of his intended Roundhouse Kick. One can see many of those excellent techniques in *Tae Kwon Do* tournaments.

Spin back into his Roundhouse Kick

The Photos below illustrate now an *offensive* application of the Kick. A good example of its use would be after your regular Front Kick on an opponent that *tends to stand his ground*. This is more of an 'in-place' jump version. But the extra power of the jump will certainly shake his confidence and his future determination to stay in place.

Drilling the offensive combination: Grounded Front Kick to Spin-back Flying Side Kick

Specific training

- Practice the *Essential* basic grounded kick (*Spin-back Side Kick*). Always practice the grounded kick *before* practicing the flying version in training.
- It is imperative to practice the kick on a marked heavy bag, from different ranges and in all its stepping form. Make sure you kick straight after the flying spin-back (Illustrated). If you do not kick straight because of a too long spinning momentum, you will graze the bag obliquely.

*Practice on the **marked** heavy bag*

- The conditioning exercise you should drill endlessly for spin-back fly-kicking excellence is the spin-jump from crouched position: Jump from the floor to the highest possible height while spinning.

Jump and Twist; higher and further

Start with 180 degrees spins, and then try to get to 360 degrees or more (See Photos).

- For precision, practice with a moving partner holding a striking pad. For full power simulation, have the partner use a thick body shield.

Use an appropriate body shield for full power partner drilling of the applied Spin-back Flying Kick

Self defense

In self-defense situations, it is usually best to be **aggressive**, as already mentioned. The set of drawings at the top of next page shows a preventive strike combination based on the step-forward technique. You confront your assailant with an aggressive full-step high punch (the basic *Oie Tsuki* of *Karate*). The step forward is slightly crooked as a preparation for the coming Spin-back. In this example, you will lead the Spin-back with a *spinning high Back-fist* or Hammer-fist Strike, both as an attack and as a protective measure. You then jump up into the Flying Side Kick. ➡

Step forward and spin aggressively to prepare the kick and to keep assailant off-balance

Illustrative Photos

Spin back airborne and kick straight!

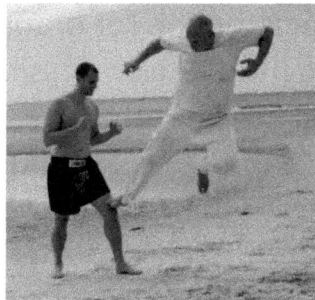

Flying Side Kicks in general can be used for devastating joint attacks

Flying Spin-back out of the centerline: from there all Spin-back Kicks are easy and relevant

The Essential classic grounded Spin-back Side Kick

7. THE DOUBLE FLYING SIDE KICK

Vôo Do Morcego (Capoeira)

General

This is an extremely acrobatic technique, typical of the more unconventional styles that are based on deception and surprise. The kick is typical of *Capoeira* practice, and we have here mentioned its Brazilian name. It is also part of the core Vietnamese *Viet-Vo-Dao* practice. Older artists will remember this kick from Catch-as-catch-can wrestling, and of course, it is always present in modern televised (fake) "wrestling" shows. We could have classified it as a Suicide Kick, as it is truly an all-or-nothing move and as landing is always problematic. It is a valid kick though for ground-fighters and acrobatic stylists, as it has the most powerful forward momentum possible. And I should add that it always comes as a surprise. Even if you do not intend to *ever* use it, like myself, the drilling of this kick will do wonders for your endurance, for your general fly-kicking and for your landing/falling confidence. Certainly nothing to sneeze at.

Description

Although the kick is rarely delivered as such, the Illustrations below show the static execution: You jump up and forward, from both feet, into a double-chambered position and then you kick. Do not forget to recoil, and land while breaking your fall, ready to roll away or keep moving. Of course, all the jumping options previously presented are relevant, especially in a dynamic execution.

Key points

- It is imperative to deliver a real kick, with chambering and immediate recoiling at impact. Otherwise, the kick turns into a push relying only on the forward momentum of the jump.
- Keep moving at the landing stage.

Targets

From the hip up all the way up to the head. This is a powerful and versatile kick: you can kick at one level or simultaneously at two different levels. You can also fly-kick down from above into a lower target like the hip joint, as often done in Vietnamese Arts (As illustrated further in the text).

Typical application

This kick lends itself better than most to a "running kick" scenario. The drawings below show the use of the kick on a retreating opponent, after blitzing him with three aggressive punches. Note that, in this application, one of the feet leaves the ground first to lead the hip twist forward. As this Twin Kick is to be used as a no-return "shock and awe" maneuver, it is best used in such blitzing overpowering attacks.

Overload him with punches,
including full-steps for momentum,
and jump up with both feet

Specific training

- Work first on your break-falls (*Ukemi*).
- Heavy bag training is imperative. Always mark the target on the bag. Make sure there are mats (*tatami*) to reception you safely, especially at first.
- Work with a partner holding focus pads or a body shield. Aim with precision for targets at different levels.

Drill target practice with a partner; kick at
different levels, kick at split levels

Self defense

The set of drawings below shows another example of the "false retreat" tactic, and the introduction of the Double Flying Side Kick *at the right moment*. You are attacked (in this case by a Reverse Punch/Front Kick combination), and choose to retreat with a large full step back. But you will rebound forward immediately into the high jump. Your Double Flying Side Kick should jam the rest of his attack or come above any developing kick.

Lure him in by retreating; rebound all out forward

Illustrative Photo

When executing the Double Flying Side Kick, it is possible, and probably recommended, to hit two targets at different heights

8. THE LOW FLYING SIDE KICK

Tiet Tuc Cuoc (Viet Vo Dao)

General

This is a kick typical of the Vietnamese styles of *Viet Vo Dao* and *Vovinam*. It is simply a Flying Side Kick aiming for the opponent's knee! This can be a very **deceptive** kick, as the high jump, or the energy displayed for the long jump, do not usually result in a low kick. That is why we have decided to present this kick separately. If delivered from high up, there is an added stomping effect on the knee. If delivered long, the strong forward momentum of the jump promises a very powerful kick. And the reader is invited to remember what Bruce Lee said about the knee joint as a target: child's play!

Description

This kick is simply a Flying Side Kick to be delivered just like the basic Flying Side Kick already encountered. Only the target is slightly out of the ordinary! Therefore, as it is delivered from a high jump, it is even more important to delay the execution of the kick itself until the last moment. And when delivered as a *long* close-to-the-floor Flying Kick, it becomes basically an Essential *but energized* Hopping front-leg Side Kick to the knee. The Figures describe the high flying version of the kick, in a rear-leg, 'kicking-leg-leaves floor-first' delivery. The **stomping** effect is clear from the use of an old tire as a practice target.

Jump high, kick low; use an impact target like a tire as an alternative to a knee joint

Key points

- As mentioned, it is even more important than with the regular Flying Side Kick to delay the *actual* kicking until the last moment, when you start coming down.
- Recoil sharply after impact, and do not let yourself be tempted to keep pushing.
- Keep your guard up: You are very close to your opponent.

Targets

The knee obviously! But also the hip joint, the thigh and even the tibia if the leg is stretched forward.

Typical application

The following Illustrations show, again, a "false retreat" tactic use of the Kick. This is because the **False Retreat** is highly suitable to Flying Kicks in general. And I love it. In this case, the tactical maneuver aims at leading an opponent *to overstretch a kick*, so as to allow you to attack his *landing* leg. When your opponent launches his Front Kick, you retreat by a full step, but rebound immediately forward to attack his landing knee with a Low Flying Side Kick. Experienced Artists will retreat just enough and just at the right speed to lure the opponent to overextend; it is all about letting him believe that he just needs to push a little more to score. The Illustrations show the rear-leg "kicking-foot-leaves-ground-first" delivery, but according to your preferences and respective positions, you could kick with the front leg and/or even jump from both feet...

Step back and rebound forward and up, to crush his knee

Specific training

- This is a kick you can drill on an **Exercise Ball,** like a *Fitness/Bossu/Swiss Ball*. The Ball can be free, stuck against a wall or hold by a partner (Illustrated).
- You can also kick an old tire hold by a partner (As illustrated at the beginning of the section), or kick a heavy bag lying on the floor.
- If practicing with a partner, be very **careful** when hitting the knee. This maneuver is potentially crippling.

Self defense

This last set of drawings shows a *long-and-low*, front-leg version with a "both-feet-leaving-ground-simultaneously" delivery. In a self-defense situation, even when surprised, it is imperative to be aggressive, especially against an armed opponent. In the example illustrated, you are suddenly confronted by an assailant, but you surprise him by an immediate pre-emptive attack. You jump at once towards him while chambering in a relatively compact state (in a 'flying ball') that keeps you relatively guarded. At the last moment, you kick down onto his front knee. As an alternative set up, you can also step away first, as if fleeing, before jumping back towards him.

A pre-emptive low and long knee Flying Kick

Illustrative Photos

Jump high and kick low with gravity's help

*The **Essential** basic Hopping Side Kick*

*The **Essential** basic Side Kick to the hip- variation of **Kantsetsu Geri** in Karatedo*

9. THE FLYING ROUNDHOUSE KICK

Mawashi Tobi Geri (Karatedo), Dtuiyu Tohllyu Chagi (TaeKwonDo), Phi Hoanh Sat Cuoc (VietVoDao), Grad Dod Te (Muay Thai), Martelo pulado (Capoeira)

General

The Flying Roundhouse Kick is easy to understand, but one should be aware of the fact that it is *not* a very powerful kick. Unless successfully and precisely targeted, the kick lacks the whipping effect that can be added when kicking from a grounded position. And the forward momentum of the jump does not add anything to the energy of the circular trajectory. It is a *fast* kick though, especially in its front-leg 'low-and-long-jump' version. In fact, it is widely used in Korean arts tournaments, because switching legs and kicking combinations are faster and easier when you are airborne. Of course, the power of the kick can be much enhanced by additional spinning maneuvers, some of which will be described later.

Description

Again, all jumping variations are relevant, but we will only describe the most common ones, all front-leg Kicks.
The Figures and Photos show a front-leg 'kicking-foot-leaves-floor-last' version, with a full (invisible) step-up and the airborne scissoring of the legs. This is probably the version that allows for maximum power, because of the airborne hip twist.

Airborne scissoring for the Flying Roundhouse Kick

The invisible step maneuver is clearly visible in this execution

The next Illustrations show the front-leg, but 'kicking-foot-leaves-floor-first' variation: the rear leg "pushes" up the kicking front leg which will then pull the rear leg further into the jump. This is, again, something akin to an **oversized** *Hopping front-leg Roundhouse Kick.*

Hopping front-leg Kick on steroids

And the following set of Drawings and Photos shows an even more *energized* version of this Hopping front-leg Roundhouse Kick. You basically jump higher *from both legs* into a very tight chambered position, and you wait for the last moment to kick. This is the front-leg but 'both-feet-leave-ground-simultaneously' Flying Roundhouse Kick.

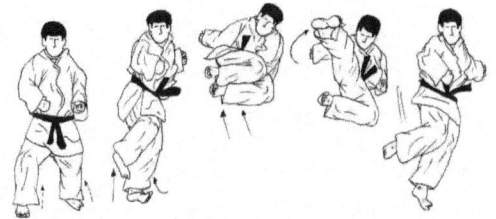

Front view of a front-leg Flying Roundhouse Kick version

Both feet leave the ground together

Rarer *Rear-leg* versions of the Flying Roundhouse Kick would usually be of the 'both-feet-leaving-ground-simultaneously' type (As will be illustrated in the coming **Typical Applications**).

Key points

- Chamber fully and keep the body in the tightest possible 'ball'.
- Wait for the last possible moment to kick.
- Kick a few inches *into* the target, but **recoil** vigorously. The Roundhouse is a 'whipping' kick.
- Keep your guard up when landing and keep on the offensive. This is usually not a single kick clincher.

Targets

The head mainly, from all sides, and the back of the neck. The upper back is also a viable target, between the shoulder blades.

Typical Applications

These Illustrations show a **rear-leg** execution of the Kick, which "*both-feet-leave-ground-simultaneously*" delivery is facilitated by a low crouching preparatory position. The example shows you facing an opponent prone to jab/cross against any perceived attack. You therefore will head-fake to provoke him, but will avoid the high jab/cross combination by lunge-stepping *forward to the outside* of your opponent while *ducking* low. It is a low and sideways evasive move. From this twisted crouched position, you seamlessly jump up to deliver a rear-leg Flying Roundhouse. The power of this kick comes from the airborne strong **hip twist**, and the target should be the back of the neck. Kick a few inches *in* and follow up.

Crouch out of the mid-line and jump up; then twist in the air for a powerful rear-leg version of the kick

The following 'Assisted' version of the Flying Roundhouse Kick really reinforces our calling these Jumping Kicks 'Sacrifice' techniques. The **Assisted** version of the Roundhouse Flying Kick is a very spectacular kick, but without the negative connotations. Spectacular could mean "unnecessarily fancy and dangerous to execute", but in this case, it also can mean "impressive and psychologically damaging to the opponent and his accomplices". This Kick, in which you use a vertical surface to climb up before executing the Roundhouse, has shown itself very effective in numerous real MMA fights, especially in the Octagon and in the cages. It is easier to execute than may seem and it definitely works. Of course, it goes without saying that it requires the right situation and set-up. In any case, it is a great kick to drill for general kicking proficiency, for situational awareness, for stamina and to keep the student's interest.

The coming photographs of the drilling of this kick will also show an important facet of **Shay Heun Karate** training: extensive outdoor training and the use of the environment as a training aid. {*Shay Heun trainees use hay bales, old tires, banana trees, sturdy trees, lakes and ponds, steep inclines, sandy beaches and much more in their regular training*}

Typical **Shay Heun***: Using a tree for an Assisted Flying Roundhouse Kick*

Using a wall for a running Assisted Flying Roundhouse Kick

Specific training

- Drill for accuracy and speed on speed ball (Illustrated).
- Drill for power and range on hanging or standing heavy bag (Illustrated).
- Always start a training session with the drilling the Essential *grounded* versions of the Full Roundhouse Kick and of the basic Front-leg Roundhouse Kick.

Accuracy- and power-drilling for the Flying Roundhouse

Drilling the 'both-feet-simultaneously' rear-leg Roundhouse Flying Kick, for power

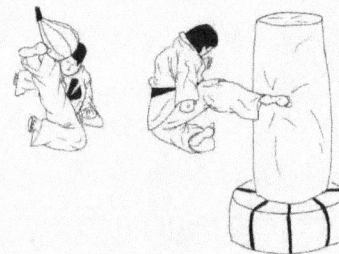

Self defense

This set of drawings describes a *low/high/low* <u>offensive</u> combination that uses surprising moves to confuse the assailant. You cause your assailant to start retreating with your Jab/rear-leg Sweep attempt (the Sweep could also be a painful low Soccer Front Kick). As you lower your leg, you immediately jump up and forward from both feet into a front-leg Flying Roundhouse Kick. Aim for the head and keep a strong forward momentum. Stay well-guarded as you land low on your bending knees. Hit him on the way down, if possible, on the shoulder or on the head with a Hammer-fist or a Back-fist Strike. Keep on the offensive by spinning back into a Low Spin-back Hook Kick to hit the back of his lower legs (turning into a double leg sweep after impact).

Hi/Lo/Flying High/Low Spin-back Sweep

Last but not least, the Illustrations below will give an example of one of the most judicious uses of the Flying Roundhouse Kick. Again, it will be jumping back at the opponent after a feinting retreat or after a small rearwards move. In the example chosen, the Flying Kick comes after releasing your caught leg from your opponent's hold; whether you have let yourself be caught on purpose as a set-up, or whether your leg has been un-willfully blocked and encircled. The release is pretty simple if you react immediately: twist the hips while spinning back and pull your leg out by sliding it with an extended ankle. As your released foot hits the ground, you jump up off both feet while continuing the spin-back you have started for the release. The Flying Roundhouse will flow naturally and strike your un-expecting opponent.

Flying Roundhouse Kick after caught-kick leg release

Illustrative Photos

The 'both-feet-leave-the-ground-simultaneously' Jump for the Flying Roundhouse

The non-kicking leg is more safely left straight for easy landing

The 'kicking-leg-leaves-the-floor-first' version

An interesting Capoeira variation in which the kick is delivered slightly downwards while you reception yourself with one hand on the ground

Flying Roundhouse Kick: Both feet leave the floor simultaneously

All Roundhouse variations can be flied: here a rear-leg 'Low Kick' straight-leg Roundhouse

Drill the basic **Essential** Roundhouse Kick before practicing the Flying versions

The Flying Roundhouse Kick in free-fighting

Drilling the hard version of the low-flying Roundhouse Kick

Rear view of an Assisted Flying Roundhouse Kick

10. THE FLYING FRONT TO ROUNDHOUSE DOUBLE KICK

General

This is probably the best possible offensive use of the Flying Roundhouse Kick: A flying combination of a Front Kick with one leg, followed by a Roundhouse Kick with the other. The Front Kick allows for a strong forward momentum and for important misdirection. And the Roundhouse caps it all with an unexpected finish in terms of target height level and direction of the incoming attack. Moreover, the "flying" part allows for a very fast leg switch. The Front Kick aims straight at the midsection, and the Roundhouse aims at the head from the side. The different levels and different angles make this kick a true *Feint Kick*. We could have presented this kick as such or as a *Double Kick* in another book, but decided otherwise: this kick is taught as a specific kick in its own right by many schools, certainly because it is so effective. It truly is a natural combination, inherently misdirecting and very much worth mastering.

Description

There are two basic ways to deliver this kick: Either (i) the Front Kick is delivered as a regular **grounded** Penetrating Front Kick, or (ii) the Front Kick is a **Flying** or at least a **Hopping** Front Kick.

The first set of Illustrations shows the delivery starting with a *grounded* Front Kick. You deliver a basic full rear-leg Penetrating Front Kick (not a feint) and you start jumping off the standing leg as soon as the kick connects. Your legs do scissor airborne and the other leg delivers the Flying Roundhouse, as the hips pivot into position.

Grounded Front kick- Top view

Grounded *Front Kick smoothly followed by Flying Roundhouse*

The second set of Illustrations shows the delivery with the Front Kick being a *Flying* Kick; or more precisely a rear-leg 'kicking-foot-leaves-ground-first' Flying Front Kick.

A long and low **Flying/Hopping** *rear-leg Front Kick followed by a Flying Roundhouse; legs scissor airborne*

Key points

- This is not a Feint Kick but a **Double Kick**: The starting Front Kick is delivered fully and aims at scoring at full power.
- The recoil from the starting Front Kick must be fast and strong and must coincide with the twisting of the hips.
- The Flying Roundhouse Kick must start from a fully and tight chambered position, and at the last possible moment.
- Make the Front Kick *low and long*, and the Roundhouse Kick *high*.

Targets

The guard, the groin or the lower abdomen for the Front Kick; the head, the neck or the shoulder blades for the Roundhouse Kick.

Typical Application

This is obviously an offensive kick that can be used with versatility. The Illustrations show a classic applied example: a simple but efficient and overpowering combination of high/high/low/high & circular. The Drawings show clearly the *high* jab/cross combination that frees the hip for the rear-leg Front Kick to the *lower* abdomen. Any credible threat to this area will get the opponent's hands down...And then comes the Flying *high* Roundhouse Kick. It is good to trust the time-tested classic combinations.

Trust the classics! Hi/Hi/Low/Hi

Specific training

- Always drill the *Essential* full-powered Penetrating Front Kick first, so as not to make it a feint in the subsequent drill.
- Working with a moving partner holding striking pads is very important. Drill full combinations with a meaningful follow-up.
- Drill on a *marked* heavy bag. You can execute with the Front Kick in the air (shadow-kicking) and the Flying Roundhouse connecting with the bag for a long kick. Or, as illustrated, you can execute the kick high and in place, with both kicks hitting the marked bag.
- A great drill for precision and range control is hitting a hanging (tennis) ball with the Front Kick, and the *marked* heavy bag behind it with the Roundhouse Kick (Illustrated). Change the distance of ball to bag for drilling shorter and longer kicks.

Drilling combinations: the Front to Flying Roundhouse Kick, followed-up by Spin-back Kick

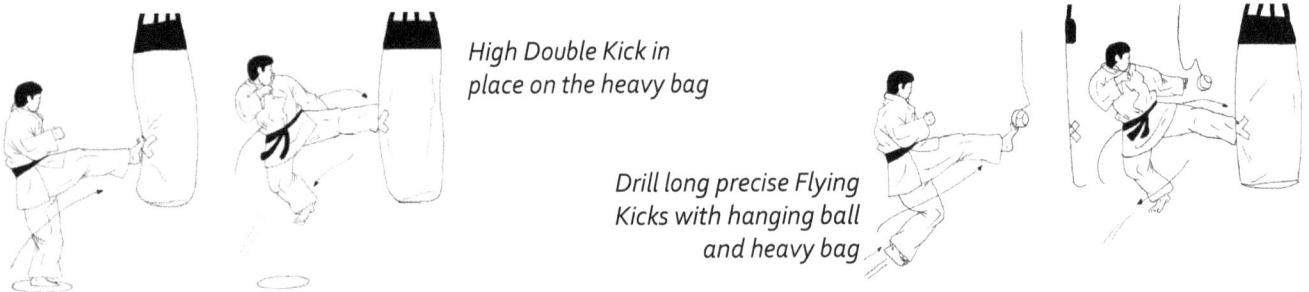

High Double Kick in place on the heavy bag

Drill long precise Flying Kicks with hanging ball and heavy bag

Self defense

This is a great kick for self-defense, especially if you make sure you score hard with *both* kicks by off-balancing him first. This kick is overpowering and aggressive, and it therefore conveys the message that you are not a victim. The Figures at the top of next page show how you feint an attack with a convincing Forward Lunge **in order to provoke a counterattack,** in this case a Front Kick Counter.

➡️

…You feint in and out, rebounding back to let him kick the void. But you explode back forward immediately with a fast Hopping front-leg Low Side Kick to the forward knee (LOW). Follow up, while lowering your kicking leg, with a fully hip-powered Cross Punch to the face (HIGH), which also pulls up your rear leg into a natural Front Kick to his *groin* (LOW). The Front Kick does not need to be that long, as you are very close to your opponent. It turns anyway into the Flying Front to Roundhouse Double Kick, hitting him hard in the head (HIGH). The Front Kick to the groin is the self-defense version of this Double Kick; if the circumstances warrant a milder attack, the Front Kick could be to the lower belly or to the solar plexus.

Front Kick to the groin and Flying Roundhouse to the head: a perfect self-defense application

Illustrative Photos

Front Kick can sometimes be an unfinished low feint,…

…but it is best executed as a fully delivered kick

11. THE DOUBLE FLYING ROUNDHOUSE KICK

General

This another suicide-like kick, just like the Double Flying Front Kick described earlier. It is acrobatic in the extreme and not very practical. This kick is even less powerful than the Double Flying Front Kick version, as the direction of the kick is not the same as the direction of the jumping momentum. But again, for acrobatic fighters, skilled in ground-fighting and looking for spectacularly surprising effects, it can be of use.

Description

The basic principle behind the kick is simple: You jump up, from both feet, in a tight coiled position with your side towards the opponent, as becomes a Roundhouse Kick. You then kick with *both* legs, chamber back forcefully and then concentrate on your landing and subsequent moving away. The following two sets of drawings will make this clearer.

There are two basic ways to deliver this kick: **(i)** Like a *front-leg* kick with the same hip staying towards the opponent; and **(ii)** the more powerful version delivered like a *rear-leg* kick with an airborne twist of the hips.

The front-leg version – Double Flying Roundhouse

The rear-leg version – Double Flying Roundhouse

Key points

- Deliver as a kick, with the whipping effect of the chamber back.
- The jump must be fully committed.
- Move away as soon as you land.

Targets

This Twin Kick must not necessarily be a high kick, but you should hit sensitive targets: the inside thigh, the groin, the kidneys, the solar plexus, the back between the shoulder blades, the head or the back of the neck.

Typical Application

The Figures show the use of the kick against a "sweeper". You avoid your opponent's committed front-leg sweep by jumping *up and forward* with your Twin Kick. The momentum of his sweep will take him into your kick (of the rear-leg type for added power). You'll reception yourself down as best as you can. As mentioned, this type of kick is great if you are from an acrobatic style, like *Capoeira* for example, and if you are a good groundfighter for following up.

Avoid the sweep by jumping up into the kick; follow up from the ground

Specific training

- Always practice your break-falls (*Ukemi*) first.
- Then, always practice the *Essential* basic Drop Double Roundhouse Kick to get the feeling of the body movement involved.
- Only after those, do start drilling the kick against the *marked* heavy bag (Illustrated at the beginning of the section), at several heights.

Self defense

The Illustrations below show the use of the kick against an aggressive assailant. Do a wide shuffle-step back on your opponent's Front Kick, but do not wait for his coming follow-up attacks (Reverse punch/Roundhouse). Rebound to jump forward in an unexpected, suicidal, but overpowering Double Flying Roundhouse Kick. Follow up.

Jump Kick to stop-crash an aggressive combination

Illustrative Photo

The Essential basic Drop Double Roundhouse Kick; a Ground Kick relative of the Double Flying Roundhouse Kick

12. THE FLYING 360 SPIN-BACK ROUNDHOUSE KICK

Tornado kick (Common name), Parafuso (Capoeira), Mom Tolyo Tshagi (Tae Kwon Do)

General

This is the first *Spinning* Flying Kick that we encounter, and it is a good example of how powerful those are. The power of these kicks, and of the Spin-back Flying Roundhouse in particular, derives nearly entirely from the centrifugal energy of the spin. The fact that these kicks are airborne allows for a faster accelerating spin and a faster hip twist, and therefore allows for more speed and more power at kicking foot level.

The 360 Spin-back Flying Roundhouse Kick, sometimes called **Tornado Kick**, is very typical of *Capoeira*, an art rich in circular movements. It is fast and powerful, but its drawbacks must be remembered as well: it inherently breaks eye contact with the opponent during the spin and the circular momentum limits the effective range. All in all, it is a very good technique, especially great as a stop/counter move when angling the jump out of the centerline.

Description

This Flying Kick is very similar to the *Essential* grounded 360 Spin-back Roundhouse Kick; it just has its 'step' airborne. It is recommended to check and drill the *grounded* Kick before attempting this flying version.

The preferred way to deliver the kick is described in the Illustrations below and the Photos at the top of next page. It is a 'kicking-foot-leaves-the-ground-last' version. The other foot (not the kicking one) leaves the ground first and executes a high spin-back *Step*. This Step is very similar to the one of the grounded kick, but it is done *airborne*. You then jump off the kicking foot while completing the full airborne maneuver: spin, chamber and kick. This variation, because of the step, allows for some *forward* range-closing movement.

The 360 Spin-back Flying Roundhouse

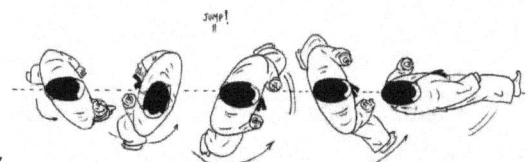

Top View

Spin back, lift knee, 'step', take-off!

The other way to deliver the kick is more difficult: it is the '*both-feet-jump*' which must achieve the full spinning momentum from the start (Illustrated below). This version is much more of a static 'in place' kick, as you pivot and jump up from both feet to twist airborne.

The second set of drawings show the *Capoeira* interpretation of this kick: it is similar to the classic version presented above, but there is much more spinning-back on the ground before take-off, and the *Capoeirista* will often have eye contact before he even starts the jump itself.

Jumping off both feet for the kick

In fact, the preparatory move before the jump could be considered a kick in itself (or at least a knee block), which **pulls** the kicking foot off the ground. This feeling of throwing first a basic Spin-back Outside Crescent Kick before jumping up, is very useful in learning to practice the full 360 Spin-back Flying Roundhouse Kick.

Spin-back with an Outside Crescent Kick; then jump up into the Flying Roundhouse

Spin back with a Knee Block; then jump up into the Flying Roundhouse

Key points

- Practice for *speed* only, not power.
- Kick *through* the target before chambering back.

Targets

This is basically a head kick. It can also be used to the back of the neck or the upper back (between shoulder blades).

Typical Applications

As already mentioned, the preferred application of this kick is an evading jump for an *angled* Stop Kick, taking you out of the centerline and catching your attacking opponent in mid-move. The Illustrations show a '*both-feet-jump-backwards-and-to-the-side*' version, launched when your opponent starts an expected Jab/Cross/Front Kick combination.

Jump up and out of the centerline

Against an opponent tending to stand his ground, a good offensive application of the kick would be to use the spinning momentum of a previous regular grounded Roundhouse Kick. In the example illustrated by the Photos below, you attack with a **kick-through** high Roundhouse Kick but you do *not* chamber back. On the contrary, you *accelerate* and use the momentum to spin-back into the Spin-back 360 Flying Roundhouse Kick. If you opponent has stood his ground or if he comes forward to counter, he will be caught by an extremely powerful Circular Kick. The Photos show the drilling of this classic combination: *Sensei Roy Faige*, head of the *Shay Heun* style, holds focus pads for one of his students.

The classic High Roundhouse Kick to Spin-back 360 Flying Roundhouse Kick combination

Of course, the principles stay the same if the opening grounded Roundhouse Kick is not the high version, but rather a Low Kick. Kick through his leg into the Spinning Flying Kick. In fact, the height difference makes this kick even more likely to succeed.

Low Kick to Spin-back 360 Flying Roundhouse Kick

Specific training

- Drill the Spinning Jump from *crouched* position, as presented in previous sections
- As advised above, practice the *grounded* Kick first.
- Drill with a *moving* partner holding striking pads
- Work the *marked* heavy bag. Mark the floor with a centerline to drill *angled* jumps.

The 360 Spin-back Flying Roundhouse; kicking leg leaves the floor last

The 'both-feet-leave-the-floor-simultaneously' version

*Drill the **Tornado Kick** on the heavy bag*

Self-defense

The aggressive combination presented in the Illustrations is counting on your opponent to try to counter-attack. After delivering a rear-leg high Roundhouse Kick, you land on purpose slightly to his *in-side*. You so offer part of your back to a counter, but you are still punching towards his face to give yourself time. As you start your spin-back, you lift your non-kicking leg in a circular **Knee Block** of his eventual counter and you jump off your kicking foot. You are in fact angling back through the centerline. You complete the spin-back and, at the last moment, deliver the full-powered 360 Roundhouse Kick to the side of his head. This maneuver is much safer than it looks, but it requires speed and therefore serious drilling.

Jump over centerline and use your raising knee to block a counter-punch

3 4 5 6

Illustrative Photos

*The Essential **grounded** 360 Spin-back Roundhouse Kick*

The Essential Spin-back Outside Crescent Kick mentioned above

13. THE FLYING BACK KICK

Ushiro Tobi Geri (Karatedo)

General

We are back to the *straight* Flying Kicks, with the Flying Back Bick; a very powerful kick, and especially efficient as a *Stop Kick*. The power derives, just like for the grounded Essential Back Kick, from the big back and gluteal muscles used in the technique. The flying version is very similar to the Flying Side Kick already encountered, but just with a little more hip twist to 'present more back' to the opponent. Of course, like with all Stop Kicks, you can jump slightly aside, slightly forwards, slightly backwards or in place, as the conditions require.

The powerful Flying Back Kick

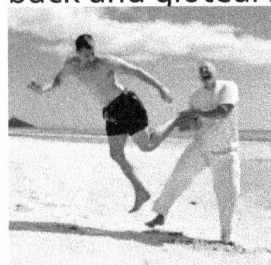
A great Stop Kick

Description

There are two basic ways to execute this kick: the rear-leg kick version and the front-leg kick version. The Illustrations below show both version.
The *first set* of drawings illustrates the **rear-leg kick**, best executed as the '*kicking-foot-leaves-floor-first*' variation. The kick is then the flying version of the Essential *Spin-forward* Back Kick. You lift the rear knee forward and start to pivot, just like for a grounded Side Kick chamber. You then jump up while keeping your airborne twist until you can deliver the Back Kick.
The *second set* shows the **front-leg delivery**. It is

The rear-leg 'Spin-forward' version of the Flying Back Kick

usually a Stop Kick, and it is best delivered, in the author's opinion, as the '*both-feet-jump*' version. You pivot <u>rearwards</u>, half-turning your back towards your opponent. Then you jump and kick with the front leg. The drawings should make everything clear.

The 'Half-spin-back' or 'front-leg' version; simply jump up and kick

Key points

- Turn the hips into a full Back Kick *starting position*; this is where the power comes from.
- Chamber fully before kicking, and *recoil* forcefully. Do not 'push'.
- Develop the kick at *last possible* moment.

Targets

Everything from upper thighs all the way to the head. The kick is very powerful and will be effective everywhere, but it lends itself better to body hits and the solar plexus should be the preferred target.

Typical Application

The Illustrations show a 'Trap' tactic, in which you purposely *cause* an attack that will in turn open your opponent to your counter-kick. The example shows a quasi-spin-back variation of the kick (it is not a *Flying* Spin-back Kick as the spin is executed on the floor!). You make a full step forward to cause your opponent to jab. But, at the last instant, you lengthen your step to his in-side to get out of the centerline and to avoid the incoming jab. By doing so, you also naturally start presenting your back to him. You do not jump yet, but cause him to start a Reverse Punch towards your offered back.

Jump off both feet to deliver a Flying Back Kick; any of your legs will work as you have your back to him.

Lure him in. Spin back on the floor, then jump-kick

Specific training

- Always practice the Essential *grounded* Spin-forward Back Kick, before the flying versions.
- Drill on the *marked* bag.
- Practice the Stop Kick with the *partner* holding a body padded shield.

Drill: protected but full-powered stop-kicking

Self defense

The Figures below show a great use of the kick against a front leg sweeper; this use also having the advantage of being irrelevant of the side the sweep is coming from. The example is in opposite guards, and your assailant attacks with an inside leg fully-committed sweep (eventually after a jab). You simply avoid the sweep by jumping off both feet, slightly rearwards, while twisting back airborne. You deliver the Back Kick with the front leg and aim for the solar plexus. You land with your back to him but can finish him off with an immediate grounded Back Kick from the other leg.

Evade a sweep by jumping directly into the Back Flying Kick

The next illustrated example shows the (almost forgotten) application of the kick delivered directly backwards. You can so overwhelm a would-be assailant coming from behind you, without having to take the time to face him. This is, in fact, the original meaning of the word 'back' in Back Kick. It is interesting to note the scissoring of the legs, which looks like a mirror image of the scissoring for a Flying *Front* Kick.

A Flying Back Kick delivered directly behind you

And if we already deal with kicking behind oneself, another example of the directly-backwards version is presented in the last set of drawings. After a classic release from a rear bear hug (Lift elbows - Butt strike rearwards - Two back circular Elbow strikes), you jump up and away while back-kicking. As you have your back towards him, you deliver the Flying Back Kick directly and with no further preparations.

Once released, jump up immediately into the kick

The Essential basic (grounded) Spin-forward Back Kick

Inaction breeds doubt and fear. Action breeds confidence and courage. If you want to conquer fear, do not sit home and think about it. Go out and get busy.
~Dale Carnegie

14. The Flying Hook Kick

General

The Flying Hook Kick is not a very practical kick in its high-flying version. It is not powerful and the jumping momentum does not add anything to the kick. But it can be of use as a 'timing' Stop Kick in certain situations. Even then, it will be usually much more practical in a 'low' hopping version.

The Flying Hook Kick is simply a higher Hopping Kick

Description

In its more useful version, the Flying Hook Kick is just an **energized** version of the Essential Hopping front-leg Hook Kick. The Illustrations and Photos show how the rear leg comes forward and pushes the kicking front leg away and up, just like for a hopping kick (but maybe a little higher). The feet do leave the floor simultaneously or at least quasi-simultaneously, and the jump can be forward, in place or rearwards.

The Flying Hook Kick is an energized Hopping Hook Kick

Key points

- Use the *twist* of the hips to give this kick some power.
- Keep your *guard up* when landing.
- Always *follow up*.

Targets

Essentially the head.

Typical Application

The Illustrations show the typical 'timing' Stop Kick application: As your opponent opens with a lunging punch and a rear-leg Front Kick, you shuffle back and immediately jump up. The jump is backwards and sideways, from both feet. You can then deliver this evading Flying Hook Kick from his blind side as he is still developing his own kick.

Jump up, back and sideways out of the centerline

Specific training

- Work the *regular* Hopping front-leg Hook Kick before any Flying Hook Kick training session.
- Drill on the *speed-ball*, as illustrated. As you have to kick through with speed, the heavy bag is unsuitable. Focus pads held by a partner are also a good training prop.

The speed-bag is a better training tool than the heavy bag: You need speed and precision

Self defense

The last Figures, at the top of next page, show the kick as something of an exotic move at the end of a combination. Attack your assailant's front shin with a *low* kick or a sweep, which will blend into a high Roundhouse Kick, ideally without touching the floor. Hitting his shin will completely divert his attention from the coming *high* kick. Kick through with the Roundhouse and lower your leg on his inside, so half-giving him your back. But you immediately jump off both feet forward. Hook-kick as you twist back towards the centerline. Follow up.

A fast and spectacular kick combination

Illustrative Photos

The Essential basic Hopping front-leg Hook Kick

Winners never quit and quitters never win.
~Vince Lombardi

15. THE FLYING SPIN-BACK HOOK KICK

Ura Mawashi Tobi Geri (Karatedo)

General

This is definitely the Spin-back Flying Kick par excellence. It is both spectacular and effective, as the speed and centrifugal energy result in a very powerful kick. It is a hallmark of *Tae Kwon Do* tournaments, where it is used a lot as a Stop Kick and where it truly shows its relevance. And, in a slightly different form, it is also a star of the hard core full-contact *Kyokushinkai* bouts. It is not, though, a kick for everybody, and it should only be used only after thorough drilling. General **Plyometric** Exercises, as well as a lot of jumping practice, are necessary for achieving excellence; thorough drilling the **spinning simple jumps**, as presented below, is especially beneficiary.

Flying Spin-back Hook Kick's effect at impact

Jump up while spinning airborne: an important basic drill for kicking excellence

Description

Like all previously described kicks, the Flying Spin-back Hook Kick can be delivered from all possible jumping variations. But we will present here the two most common and practical versions.

The first set of Figures, *at the top of next page*, shows the very classic delivery with the rear leg-kicking, just like with the *Essential* regular *grounded* Spin-back Hook Kick. You start twisting in place, just like for the grounded version, but jump up somewhere around having your back facing the opponent. You can jump up from both feet or with the kicking foot (rear-leg) first, as most comfortable to your delivery. Keep spinning and deliver the Hook Kick **through** the target with no slowing down. ➡

*Spin back; jump off both feet; keep spinning
while delivering the Hook Kick*

The next Figures and Photos, *below*, show the kick delivered with the **front** leg. This is a more aggressive move which involves an *invisible step-up* forward with the rear leg: you lift the rear foot forward and up while starting to pivot. You then kick off the previously front leg (the kicking leg), helping yourself by mentally pushing from the '**invisible step**'. Keep twisting and spinning, and deliver the kick *through* the target. The drawings make this clearer.

The more aggressive front-leg Spin-back Hook Kick

Dynamic delivery of Flying Spin-back Hook Kick with the front leg

Key points

- This is a *speed* kick: keep muscles relaxed.
- Kick *through* the target; do not slow the kick towards impact.

Targets

The head mainly.

Typical Application

Like most Spinning Flying Kicks, the best way to use the Flying Spin-back Hook Kick is as a *'timing' Stop Kick*. The illustrated example shows how you provoke an attack by stepping forward with an out-of-range Punch. You then keep the momentum to jump **forward and obliquely** out of the centerline. You so can intercept your opponent's incoming counter-attack Front Kick with your own Flying Spin-back Kick.

Stop-kick a counter that you have provoked; jump away from the centerline

Specific training

- Drill hopping, jumping and *spin-jumping*.
- Always practice the regular *grounded* Spin-back Hook Kick, before drilling the flying version. Go from grounded to grounded-in-movement, then to hopping and then to flying.
- Deliver the kick in all three variations: *in place, forward and backwards*.
- Drill the forward-jumping kick by kicking the marked heavy bag while jumping over an *obstacle* like a lying bag (Illustrated).

Drill the forward momentum with the help of obstacles

Self defense

The last drawings show, again, a 'timing' Stop Kick. In this example, you will be jumping backwards when attacked. Your assailant attacks with a classic Reverse Lunge Punch and prepares to follow up with a Roundhouse Kick. You shuffle back and then jump rearwards and obliquely (off both feet) while starting your airborne spinning. Being out of the centerline, you will be able to catch him in the head before he completes his kick. Remember that the start of your rearwards move is all about luring him in.

Lure him in by retreating just enough; jump off-centerline to catch him into his attack

The Essential **grounded** *Spin-back Hook Kick*

Another execution of the basic Spin-back Hook Kick

16. THE FLYING CRESCENT KICK

Mikazuki Tobi Geri (Karatedo)

General

The Flying Crescent Kick, -in its full name Flying **Inside** Crescent Kick-, is a very useful kick. It is fast and powerful; especially in its *front-leg step-up* form. The Kick is much stronger than the Flying *Outside* Crescent Kick, because the hip movement needed is in sync with the jump. The Kick also climbs up towards its target mostly out of sight, and it can therefore be very surprising. The Kick is quite easily mastered and does not require extreme flexibility. The Kick can also be delivered, -just like the regular *grounded* Crescent Kick-, in either a narrow or a wide arc as the circumstances dictate. A very versatile technique indeed.

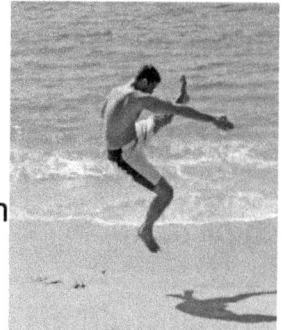

Typical Flying Inside Crescent Kicks – Dotan De Bremaeker

Description

The first Illustrations show the kick delivered **with the rear leg**: the kicking rear-foot leaves the floor *slightly before* or *just together* with the front foot for a classic Crescent Kick, but executed airborne. You can jump high or long, as needed.

Rear-leg Flying Crescent kick; front view

The second set of drawings shows my preferred version of the kick: a long forward-jumping **front-leg** kick which is following an *airborne step-up*. Bring your rear foot up and forward, as if stepping on an *invisible* stool in front of you to help you jump off the kicking foot. Throw the kick while airborne with a full hip twist. One of the advantages of this delivery option is that the step-up can be made look like the start of a Front Kick, which will lure your opponent into blocking down.

Front-leg Flying Crescent Kick; the invisible step method

Key points

- You must kick with the *hip*, not the leg.
- Kick *through* the target and try *not* to to slow when touching the target.
- Keep your *guard up*, as you kick and land very close to your opponent.

Targets

Primarily the head. But also the guarding limbs, the upper torso, the back of the neck and between the shoulder blades, as a well-executed kick is rather powerful.

Typical Application

The Illustrations show the use of the kick as something of a **Feint Kick**: you'll purposely make the *step-up* look like a Front Kick for as long as possible. Your opponent will block down and out, while you will be coming in and up. This will work best if you have already delivered at least one real Front Kick. In the example, you thus take the offensive with a Front Kick to the lower abdomen and then land forward while reverse-punching, again to the body. The Reverse Punch will help pull your hip naturally for a rear-leg Front Kick Chamber. You extend the leg for as long as possible in a front-kick-look-alike, *before turning into a long Step-up*. You then jump off the kicking leg in a **long** forward hop while delivering the Crescent Kick to his head.

Make the "invisible" Step-up look like an incoming Front Kick

Specific training

- Drill the *Essential* Hopping front-leg Crescent Kick and increase gradually the height and length of the hop.
- Work the forward jump by drilling the kick on the marked bag while jumping over an *obstacle* like a lying bag, as Illustrated.

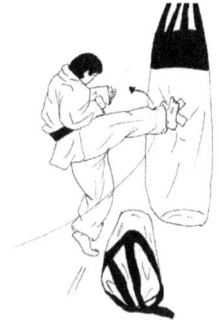

Drill the kick over an obstacle

Self defense

Another typical application of the Flying Kicks, already encountered, is their use against committed Low Kicks to your legs or against full-powered Sweeps. The Figures show the use of the *Flying Inside Crescent Kick* against an attempted sweep of your front leg. You will jump up and forward from both feet to evade the sweep, and deliver the *rear-leg* Crescent Kick to his incoming head.

Jump off both feet to evade a sweep; crescent-kick

You will never do anything in this world without courage. It is the greatest quality of the mind next to honor.
~Aristotle

17. THE FLYING OUTSIDE CRESCENT KICK

General

The Flying *Outside* Crescent Kick is not a very powerful kick, as the hip movement is not naturally strong in the direction used. But, -especially in its energized hopping version-, it is fast and can be surprising because of his angling vector. Also, a well-executed kick is out of the field of vision of the opponent for most of its trajectory. If you make sure to follow up, it is therefore a useful technique.

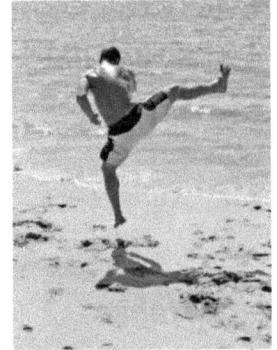

Typical Flying Outside Crescent Kick

Description

The most practical delivery of the kick is the *front-leg* delivery, with the kicking foot leaving the ground last. You will again realize that it is basically an *Essential* **Hopping** front-leg regular Outside Crescent Kick, just slightly higher and slightly longer. The kick can be delivered with more or less energy, as the circumstances dictate. The first set of drawings shows the "light" version, very much the energized Hopping delivery, with the back leg coming forward to "push up" the kicking front leg. The second set shows the *more energetic version*, with the rear leg stepping all the way forward for

The front-leg Flying Outside Crescent kick; an supersized Hopping Kick

an **invisible step-up**, leading into an airborne 'rear-leg' Outside Crescent Kick. This version allows for more hip twist into the kick, and therefore for more power.

The front-leg Flying Outside Crescent Kick; start with a rear-leg Front Kick chamber as a step-up

Key points

- Lift the kicking foot as *close to the opponent's body* as possible, in order to keep it out of his vision field.
- Keep your *guard up* as you are very close to the opponent.
- Do not slap, but *kick through* the target.

Targets

Essentially the head.

Typical Application

As you already know, I am a fan of the use of Flying Kicks as Stop Kicks. And I am a strong believer in **angling** and in evading sideways. The Illustrations show a 'shuffle-back-and-rebound-forward' maneuver against a Lunge Punch/Hopping Front Kick attack. As your opponent lunges from opposite guard, you shuffle back to give him confidence. But your retreating rear leg rebounds forward to allow for a jump *up, forward and to your in-side*. You then deliver the Flying Outside Crescent Kick from slightly *out of the centerline* while he attempts to follow up with his planned front-leg Kick.

Lure him in by jumping back, then rebound forward and out of the centerline; jump-kick

Specific training

- This is a fast kick that needs to go *through* the target; it needs to be drilled on the speed ball or a similar light target, preferably **not** on the heavy bag. A partner holding a focus pad is great.
- Practice the *Essential grounded* front-leg Outside Crescent Kick first. Then increase the *hopping* gradually until you deliver a full Flying Kick.

Drill the kick on a target you can kick through

Self defense

The Figures at the top of next page show an offensive combination, great to be used after getting your opponent used to a pattern of low front-kicking. You and your partner exchange prodding Front Kicks that back rearwards each time, in order to 'feel' one another at the start of a fight. You then block, again, a short Front Kick by your assailant, and you respond in the predictable manner with your own rear-leg Front Kick. But this time you will land forward. You then try to control his blocking lowered arms while jumping up slightly to your inside. You can now deliver a high Flying Outside Crescent Kick to the side of his head.

Get your opponent used to a pattern, then break it

Illustrative Photos

The Essential basic Outside Crescent Kick

Drilling the basic Outside Crescent Kick

Front-leg Essential Hopping Outside Crescent Kick at impact – Roy Faige

18. THE FLYING SPIN-BACK CRESCENT KICK

Meia-lua de frente pulada, Parafuso (Capoeira)

General

This kick is the airborne version of the Spin-back Crescent Kick, and, like its grounded counterpart, it is very powerful as it gathers speed during a full 360 spin. Of course, the full spin goes hand in hand with a long delivery time and with the loss of eye contact, which makes it a kick to use only under the suitable circumstances. But an added advantage of the kick is that the chambered rear-leg knee gives some protection during the spin-back, as something of a sweeping Knee Block. In any case, this is an important kick to drill for overall Flying Spinning Kicks proficiency.

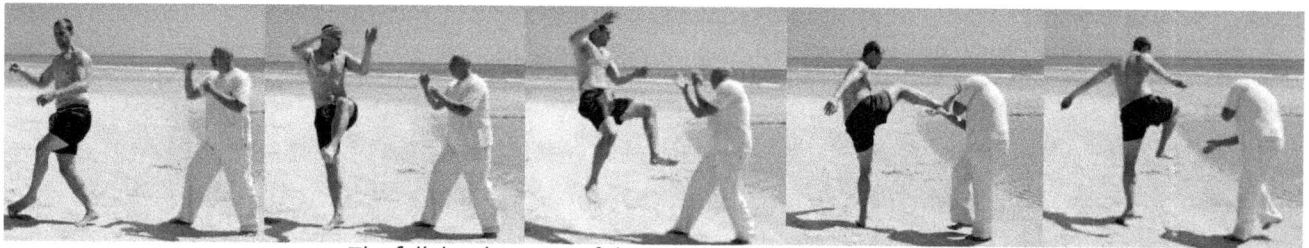

The full development of the Spin-back Flying Crescent Kick

Description

The Drawings and Photos are worth a thousand words, and as mentioned, the kick is very similar to the *Essential grounded* basic 360 Spin-back Crescent Kick. You start by spinning back and lifting the rear foot. But you then jump off the kicking foot while continuing the spin. You can now complete the forward 'step' with the rear leg in the air, before throwing the Crescent Kick.

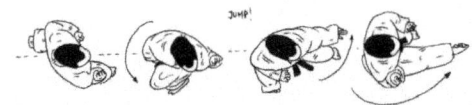

Top view of the kick

The Spin-back Flying Crescent Kick

The Flying Spin-back Crescent Kick is very similar to the grounded version of the kick

Key points

- Jump up in a spinning rear-leg Step-up. Only then, and *at the last minute*, do you complete the Crescent Kick. It is the length of the step that will define the range.
- Kick *through* the target: this is a momentum kick driven by acceleration.
- Keep your *guard up* as you are very close to the opponent.
- Minimize the loss of *eye contact*.

Targets

Preferably the head. But as it is a powerful kick, guarding hands, sternum, even shoulders and upper back between the shoulder blades are worthy targets.

Typical Application

The Drawings show another key opportunity, already encountered, for the natural use of Flying Kicks: when you have lowered yourself onto bent legs for a tactical reason, like ducking. In such a situation, you have a power spring-up advantage, the effect of surprise and the opportunity for a low/high combination. In the example illustrated below, -ducking under a full powered rear-leg Roundhouse Kick-, you have the added advantage of being on his blindside.

Duck below a high kick and jump up into a Flying Kick

Specific training

- Drill the jumping spins from *crouched* position, as already presented and illustrated several times. Aim to complete more than a 360 degrees spin.
- Practice on the heavy bag, on the *speed bag* and with a partner holding focus pads.
- Always start your drilling with the *grounded* version of the kick, gradually going to Hopping and then to Jumping.

Self defense

The last drawings show an aggressive lo/hi combination which purpose is to overwhelm your opponent with a full one-and-a-half circle attack. As soon as your assailant seems intent to start his attack, you launch a full powered rear-leg (**low**) Roundhouse Kick to his kidneys. This is a *Sen-no-sen* (intuitive pre-emptive) attack and a fully committed hip-powered 'Low Kick'. You chamber and lower the leg forward and *to your in-side*. You are already giving half your back to the opponent, but you are also in a good position to *continue spinning*. By keeping the twist going, you are in fact thwarting any counter that your hurt opponent could have been launching. You complete the full Flying Spin with the (**high**) Crescent Kick to his unprotected face.

Low Roundhouse Kick followed by high Spin-back Flying Crescent Kick: A full one-and-a-half circle

Illustrative Photos

*The **Essential** grounded basic 360 Spin-back Crescent Kick*

A more detailed applied grounded 360 Spin-back Crescent Kick

19. THE FLYING SPIN-BACK OUTSIDE CRESCENT KICK

Armada pulada (Capoeira)

General

This is probably the most practical of the Spinning Flying Kicks for the widest array of fighter types. It is fast and the inherent foot trajectory keeps it hidden for longer than the Flying Spin-back Hook Kick for example. The acceleration of the Spin-back Jump gathers enough energy to give a very powerful, fast and deceptive kick. It is also probably the easiest Flying Spinning Kick to master. This great kick is very much used by *Capoeiristas*, and they even have a spectacular variation in which they kick with both feet together (*Armada Dupla*), although we shall not present it here, as certainly too acrobatic for most Artists outside this particular style.

Description

The kick is very similar to the Essential *grounded* version of the Spin-back Outside Crescent Kick. You do a full Spin-back in place *and then jump up* off both feet more or less simultaneously, to keep the spin on. You keep twisting airborne and deliver the kick **through** the target, very much like for the corresponding grounded kick. Refer to the coming Figures and Photos.

The Spin-back Outside Crescent Flying Kick

Top view of the kick

Spin and jump, then kick

Key points

- The *hips* are driving the kick, not the leg.
- The transition from spinning to jump-spinning is seamless: it is the same one move. *No transition*. Think of delivering the grounded Kick with a slight hop to get closer.
- *Minimize the loss of eye contact*. Turn the head first, then the shoulders, then the hips. You jump when you are already watching your opponent from over your shoulder.
- Kick *through* the target. This is an acceleration kick, not to be slowed at impact.

Targets

This is mostly a head kick. You could consider also the guarding arms, the sternum and the shoulder blades.

Typical Application

This kick is the perfect follow-up to any action starting with a pivot, especially from a close range. All experienced artists know that the best way to counter a circular kick is to get close to the pivotal axis during the execution of the kick, as the centrifugal energy is minimal there. The power is at its highest far away, at the foot extremity. The Illustrations show an application in which the beginning of the Spin-back is an evasive maneuver towards the axis of the opponent's kick. The Spin-back Outside Crescent Flying Kick will be used after blocking a (grounded) Spin-back Hook Kick by inching forward and pivoting *into* the kick, to reach the closest to the center of gravity of the kicker. This application would be valid against a front-leg Hook Kick, a Side Kick, a Back Kick and more. You then make use of the pivot momentum to enter into jump-spinning and into the Kick itself. You should ideally connect with the back of his neck. As you should normally land at your opponent's back, a good follow up would be a Stomp Kick to the back of his knee while keeping control of his arms for added security.

Evade forward and spin-jump into his circular kick

Specific training

- This is a kick to practice with a partner holding *focus pads*. It is difficult to practice on the speedball, and unnecessary to drill on the heavy bag.
- Always start by drilling the *grounded* version of the Spin-back Outside Crescent Kick. Then start to slightly hop, and increase the height and length of the hop gradually.

Self defense

The Drawings show an aggressive use of the kick in a blasting combination, where you spin twice while continuously firing attacks to overwhelm your opponent. You start with a lunging *high* Reverse Punch that will naturally pull your rear leg forward into a *Low* Soccer Front Kick to his front shin. You lower your foot forward and out, and then spin back into a *Low* Spin-back Hook Kick to the *same* leg. You complete your spin, keeping your hands up, both as a protection and to keep his attention up. You seamlessly repeat the same *low* Soccer Kick and go into a second spin-back, making sure it looks like the previous combination. He will expect, again, an attack to his shin or knee! But, this time, you will *jump up in the high* Flying Spin-back Outside Crescent Kick. **Hi/Lo/Lo/Lo/ Flying High !**

Attrition to his shin, followed by unexpected high Flying Kick

20. THE DOUBLE FLYING SPIN-BACK OUTWARD CRESCENT TO CRESCENT KICK

The Butterfly Kick (Common name)

General

This is an acrobatic and very special kick, definitely not for everybody. I have, though, seen it used in competitive sport, and must therefore consider it a serious option for the skilled practitioner in some situations. The reader is invited to take into account though, that, most of the time, the kicker ends on the floor after delivery. A successful kick will, of course be very surprising and very effective, as this Double Kick has the centrifugal energy advantages of the Flying Spinning Kicks. The spinning momentum and the hip movement of both kicks complete each other, and the "scissoring" of the legs does give an extra power boost. Needless to add that the kick is very spectacular, which is sometimes of serious psychological importance.

Description

The first half of the kick is totally a Spin-back Flying Outside Crescent Kick, as described in previous sections. But once you approach the target with the Outside Crescent, you start moving the body differently: the other leg, instead of getting ready to come down, uses the hip momentum to go up into an *Inside* Crescent movement. The Illustrations and Photos show clearly that, as the first kick goes through the target at the apex of its trajectory and starts its descent, the other leg goes up in a wide **scissor-like** movement for a full blown *Crescent Kick*.

Front and Top view of the Butterfly Kick

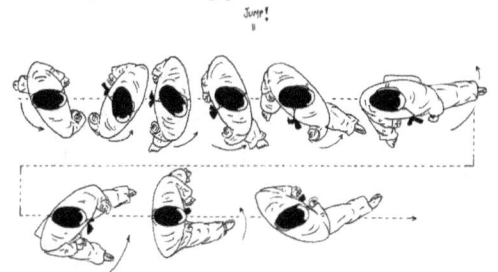

The Double Flying Spin-back Outward Crescent to Crescent Kick a.k.a Butterfly Kick

Key points

- This is a high and complex Flying Kick: you need to jump as *high* as possible.
- Kick *through* with *both* kicks and do not slow the momentum before the second kick has hit *through* the target. This is why the practitioner often has to reception himself on the ground after the kick.
- The first kick (Outside Crescent) is a *full-powered* kick and not a feint. In fact, it pulls in the second kick.

Targets

This is essentially a head kick.

Typical Applications

In order for the kick to succeed, you need to be close to the opponent and you need to control him for as long as possible while you prepare the kick. The first set of Illustrations show how it can start with the Outside Block of a full-step Lunge Punch, from opposite stances. The Block, in traditional Cat Stance, allows for the control of the opponent from the outside and for the beginning of the Spin-back in the same circular direction. Jump up and deliver the Double Kick to the opponent's head. Land as best as can and keep fighting, from the ground if necessary.

Start pivot while blocking from the out-side; then double-kick

The drawings at the top of net page show a variation of the Kick as it is practiced in *Capoeira*, where the Flying Crescent Kick is more of an hybrid Roundhouse Kick. This kick, called '*Martelo Rodado Voador*' is more powerful; but it requires an additional airborne hip twist, which makes it more acrobatic and more difficult to perform. The *Capoeira* style relies much on circular movements; note from the Illustrations how the head and the shoulders "pull" much more the hips into the kick than in Japanese styles for example. The Capoeirista will kick through the target and keep rotating for more kicks and this is what makes it pretty unique. In the example, the second kick is a hybrid of a Crescent Kick and of a Straight-leg Roundhouse Kick, which connects with the top of the ankle after a powerful hip pull.

Capoiera's Martelo Rodado Voador

Specific training

- Start drilling the Essential *grounded* Spin-back Outside Crescent Kick. Then drill the Flying version presented earlier in this book. Only after warming up with those two, should you proceed to the "Butterfly Kick".
- Work with a partner holding a *focus pad* that is to be hit with both feet in sequence (Illustrated).

This kick is best drilled on striking pads held by a partner

Self defense

The drawings show an offensive use of the Kick after having softened the assailant up with an attack which prepares the Spin-back Jump. You open with a **low** Front Soccer Kick/**high** Roundhouse same-leg combination. You lower the kicking while twisting already. It turns into a Spin-back and you jump up into the Butterfly Kick. If you land on your hands and feet after kicking through, it is best to keep the circular momentum going. Follow up with an *Essential* basic Hand-on-ground Spin-back Hook Kick, for example. It should be mentioned that the low kick at the beginning of the combination is mostly a *Feint Kick*. It can be a full kick if possible, but it can also be a "*Leg Tap*" that will divert the opponent's attention from the developing follow-up, even if for an instant. This type of feint is very effective, because the **contact** itself will provoke more of an unconscious reaction than a feinting move that does not end in a physical touch.

The Butterfly Kick with opening combination and with follow-up from the ground

Illustrative Photos

Essential Body-bent Spin-back Hook Kick

Essential Hand-on-floor Spin-back Hook Kick

Essential Drop Spin-back Hook Kick

21. The Flying Spin-back Downward Heel Kick

General

This is a useful kick: fast, powerful and surprising. This is also the kick you will switch to if your Flying Spin-back Outside Crescent Kick is on course to miss a ducking or crouching opponent. It is also somewhat easier to perform than the Spin-back Flying Outside Crescent Kick itself, as the "amount" of flying spin is smaller. In fact, it is as if you deliver the Flying Outside Crescent to 3/4 of the full spin, *and then* deliver a regular Downward Heel Kick (*Axe Kick*) while coming down and completing the spin on inertia. It is clearly not a pure Downward Heel Kick as it comes *diagonally* down on account of the spin.

This complex kick is unique in the Flying Kicks' realm, by way of the fact that you should aim at hitting the target *together with the landing of the non-kicking foot* (See Photo). Of course, like with many Flying Kicks, you should be aware of the possibility that you will end up on the ground after scoring. In any case, always follow up.

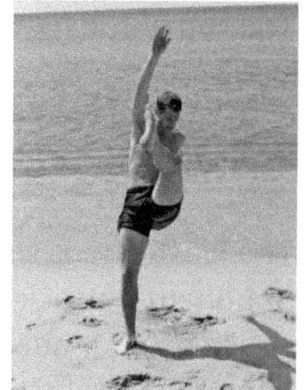
Spin-back Flying Downward Heel Kick: Connect down just as you land

Description

The Kick is clearly illustrated by the Figures below. As mentioned, you start with a spin that would allow you to deliver a *high* Spin-back Flying Outside Crescent Kick to an opponent at your **9 o'clock**. You then keep spinning towards **12 o'clock** *while lowering forcefully your foot downwards* into the target, in a diagonal airborne Axe Kick move. You lower the non-kicking leg to try to land as close as possible to the moment of impact, both for balance reasons and for power maximization. The Kick is, in some way, an *energized* Hopping version of the Essential Spin-back Downward Heel Kick.

The Spin-back Flying Downward Heel Kick

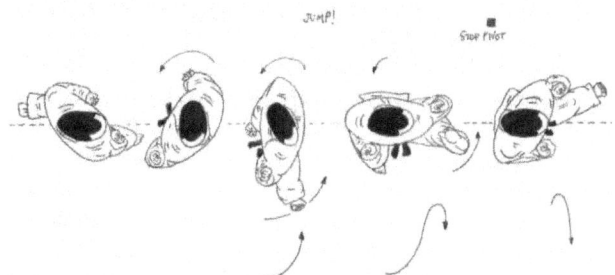
Top view of the kick: Note the start of the downward move

Key points

- The kicking foot should reach its apex just after *crossing the 3/4 spin*.
- This is an example of a Spinning Kick in which the spinning momentum should be *slowed* (when the foot starts coming down). Exception to the general rule.
- This is a downward high kick: you need to jump *high*.

Targets

The top of the head, the clavicle. Also the neck and back of a bent-over opponent.

Typical Application

The Illustrations show the use of the kick as a '*timing*' Stop Kick, after provoking your opponent's attack by a purposefully opened guard (*Trap Tactic*). In opposite stance, you keep your guard up to open your midsection to the Front Kick that you know your opponent is fond of. This is an inviting trap, difficult to resist. As he delivers the expected kick, you spin back and *jump up obliquely* out of the centerline. Your downward heel will catch him while he lowers the leg and while he is still off-balance and committed.

As he starts his move, commit yourself to an oblique Spin-back Jump out of the centerline. Axe-kick down

Specific training

- Drill the *grounded* Spin-back Downward Heel Kick. Start hopping, and then gradually increase the jump.
- Practice with a *partner* holding a focus pad as illustrated.

Best to be drilled with focus pads: Kick through

Self defense

The Drawings show the use of the Kick on an assailant bent-over by a previous attack to the groin, in this case by a Roundhouse. <u>Such a technique is dangerously powerful and should be used with extreme caution</u>. The example shows an inversion of momentum between the groin Roundhouse going one way, and then the Spin-back Jump going the other way. The switch may seem unpractical. *It should be clear that it is definitely not*: it is a surprising tactic, which works extremely well, and that can be applied to other circular kicks; its general drilling is warmly recommended. In this specific example, you are threatened by an assailant lifting a stick to attack you. Instead of retreating as he expects, you deliver a *fast* Roundhouse (in this example, rear-leg) to his open groin. You lower the leg forcefully rearwards to start your spinning-back jump in the *opposite* direction to the Roundhouse. Your Flying Downward 'Axe' Heel Kick should aim for the exposed back of his neck, if the situation warrants it (**CAUTION in training**).

Spin-back Flying Downward Heel Kick to the exposed back of the neck: an extremely dangerous technique

Illustrative Photos

The Essential grounded Spin-back Downward Heel Kick

An application of the basic grounded Spin-back Downward 'Axe' Heel Kick

22. THE FLYING 360 SPIN-BACK DOWNWARD HEEL KICK

General

This is basically the previous kick (Flying Spin-back Downward Heel Kick) but delivered *with the front leg and after an airborne full step forward*. The various possible footwork and steps leading to a Flying Kick have to be executed in a way that is conducive to the momentum of the kick, and therefore they are not necessarily standard. This is why we present here this variation, which is simply a different setting up for the previous kick. It is to be noted that the same variation could be applied, for example, to the Spin-back Flying Outside Crescent Kick already encountered (although it will not be presented here in detail, the principles are identical and the experienced Artist will have no problems in applying them).

The Flying 360 Spin-back Downward 'Axe' Heel Kick is a very powerful kick because of the acceleration during a full spin. It has the added benefit of the initial **airborne step** being a protective circular knee-block. Of course delivery time is long and you do loose eye contact during the spin. It is an interesting technique though, and which principles can be extended to other Spinning Flying Kicks.

The landing of a 360 Flying Spin-back Downward Heel Kick

Description

You bring your rear knee forward while initiating a circular twisting movement, very much like that of an *Essential* rear-leg Side Kick but where you keep pivoting. This is basically a **Spin-forward** move. You then jump off the previously front leg, as high as possible, while keeping the momentum that has now become a **Spin-back**. You lift this leg as high as possible in an Outside Crescent Kick motion, and you aim to reach apex at your 9 o'clock. You keep twisting airborne and start the Downward Heel Kick towards your 11 o'clock. You complete the kick while winding down the spin and while landing on the other leg. The Illustrations are worth a thousand words.

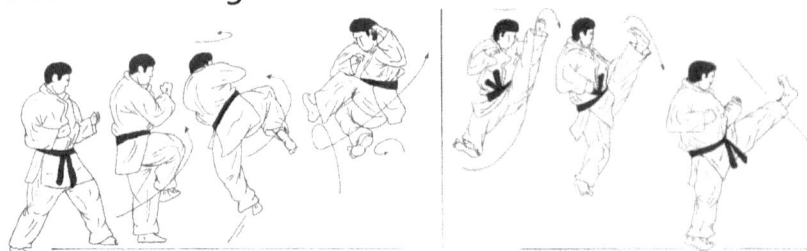

The spectacular Flying 360 Spin-back Downward Heel Kick

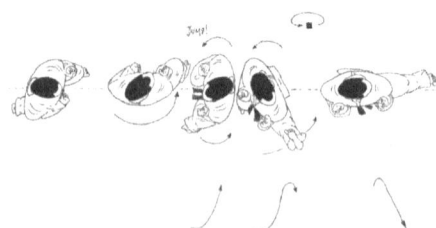

Top view of the kick

Key points

- Just like for the regular kick, you have to jump *high* and to plan for *landing* simultaneously with the kick impact
- Keep your *guard up* during the initial step forward.
- It is the initial *knee lift* that gives the impetus for the spin: lift high, round, fast and with full commitment.

Targets

Head and collar bones. Neck and back if the opponent is bent-over.

Typical Application

The Figures show an interesting application of the kick, in which you use the first "step-up" to deliver a *Flying Circular Knee Strike* into your opponent's thigh muscle. In the example presented, you are attacked with a Reverse Punch/rear-leg Full Roundhouse Kick combination. You jump up *into* the kick with a rear-leg Circular *Knee Strike* into the upper thigh muscles of your opponent's raising leg. You 'knee through' and keep the spinning/flying momentum in order to deliver the Downwards Heel Kick to the side of his neck as he stumbles back from his unsuccessful kick.

Use the start of the Kick to block an incoming kick and keep the twisting momentum until completion

Specific training

- Drill the Essential *grounded* Spin-back Downward Heel Kick, and then the flying version. Only then should you start to practice, with a *gradual step-up*, the Flying 360 Spin-back version of the kick.
- Practice with a partner holding *two focus pads*, the first one for the "knee strike", and the second for the Downward Heel Axe Kick, as illustrated.

Drill the kick on focus pads held by partner; kick through

Self defense

In the application illustrated, the initial knee movement is purposely used to brush off an incoming Reverse Punch *that you have provoked*. As shown, you invite a classic Reverse Counter Punch by feinting half-a-Reverse Punch of your own followed by a time-out. You then can jump up into the kick, starting by knee-blocking his incoming punch and finishing up with the Downward Heel Axe Kick after a full spin.

Tease a counter-puncher and block him with the 'Knee-Block' phase of the kick

There may be people that have more talent than you, but there is no excuse for anyone to work harder than you do.
~Derek Jeter

23. THE FLYING SPIN-BACK BACK KICK

General

The Flying Spin-back Back Kick, like all Back Kicks, is very powerful because of the big muscles involved (back muscles and gluteus). It is a useful kick, especially good to use as a Stop Kick or as a Counter. It could be deemed somewhat surprising because the Spin-back Jump is usually the indicator of a circular kick, and not of a straight 'stopping' one. That is why this kick could be better described, for conceptualization, as a *Spin-back Jump* first which purpose is to bring you to an airborne coiled position with your back towards your opponent. From this **end-position**, there will be *no more spinning*. You just 'happen' to kick backwards from there at the last minute, just before starting your descent. It is all in the mind...

The Flying Spin-back Back Kick

Description

As shown in the Illustrations, you jump up, *preferably from both feet*, and you start your spin-back in such a way that it **stops** at 180 degrees. From the airborne-chambered position, you deliver a classic *Essential* Back Kick.

Simple but powerful: The Flying Spin-back Back Kick

Key points

- Like for the Essential grounded Spin-back kick, it is imperative to totally *switch from a circular to a straight movement*: Jump up for half-a-spin and no more.
- Kick *at the last moment*, just before starting your landing.
- *Chamber back* the kicking leg forcefully after impact, like for any Back Kick

Targets

This is a **powerful** kick: everything on the head and body. Even the shoulders and the guarding limbs are worthwhile targets.

Typical Application

This is, like most Flying Kicks, a good move against Circular Kicks, which momentum tends to place your opponent off-balance or off-guard. The Illustrations show you feinting in and out (from opposite stances) to provoke a Spin-back Hook Kick that you'll avoid with a rear body evasion. While he completes his Circular Kick momentum, you jump up into the Spin-back. You deliver the Back Kick to his sternum as he is lowering his leg. You keep the pressure and your forward momentum after landing. Start with a *high* Back-fist strike as he keeps retreating and then keep him off-balance by kicking *low*. In this case, we have illustrated a groin Hook Kick that flows naturally into his retreating step. Of course, this is an example only; the follow-up will have to adapt to the situation and to the opponent's reactions.

Provoke a Spin-back Hook Kick that you evade and spin-back-jump-kick straight into his landing

Specific training

- As illustrated at the top of next page, drill the 180 degrees jumps from crouched position. Strive to do *exactly half-a-turn*, not more, not less.
- Always start by practicing the Essential basic *grounded* Spin-back Back Kick. Then start lightly hopping while kicking. Increase the hop gradually into a jump.

...

- Practice the kick on the heavy bag, with two *hurdles* on the sides which will force you to kick *straight* and not diagonally. This will teach you to avoid the spinning inertia. The hurdles could be standing bags, like in the Figure, or chairs, or ladders or even partners.

Use props to train to kick straight after the spin-back

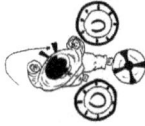

Drill 180 degrees jumps

- Another way to achieve good control is to practice on a (slowly) *moving opponent* holding a body padded shield: If the kick is not straight, it will slip on the shield.

Drilling with a partner is essential

Self defense

The offensive combination presented in the Drawings shows the use of the kick after an overpowering blast. The idea is that, -after exclusively **high** attacks-, the kick is directed at the **body,** all the while a feint to the head keeps his hands high. The example goes as follows: you first launch a *high* Lunging Punch/*high* Spin-back Hook Kick combination. As your assailant retreats, you land with another *high* Lunging Jab, and you keep the momentum into another immediate Spin-back. But this time you jump up with the twist. Your assailant has been reinforced in expecting another *high* attack. While spin-back-flying, you therefore feint a *high* Spinning Punch towards his head (that also helps the spinning). But in fact you deliver, at the last moment, the Flying Back Kick to his exposed *body*.

Lower belly Flying Spin-back Back Kick after a series of overpowering high attacks

3   4   5   6   7

*The Essential **grounded** Spin-back Back Kick: a powerful kick indeed*

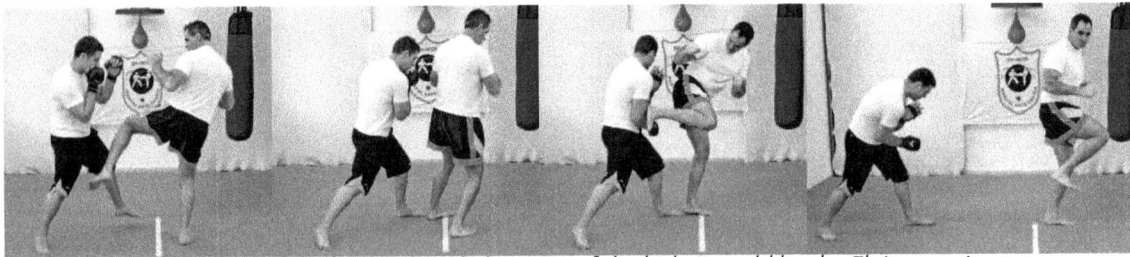

An application of the basic grounded version of the kick; it could be the Flying version too

Another classic application of the Essential grounded version of the Kick; it could be the Flying version as well

You have to expect things of yourself before you can do them."
~Michael Jordan

24. THE DOUBLE FLYING BACK KICK COMBINATION

General

This is a very interesting **Double Kick,** looking acrobatic but surprisingly easy to perform. It is also very efficient as an overpowering aggressive maneuver. It is a classic Flying Back Kick (as just described in the previous section), but followed by *another* **airborne** Back Kick with the other leg. Back Kicks being inherently powerful, this technique, often executed as a *Running Kick,* delivers an impressive double whammy to the opponent. Unlike most Double Kicks, this combination ensures two equally powerful kicks, because of the unique straight momentum: everything is going in the same direction. The second kick, being usually unexpected, tends to hurt even more.

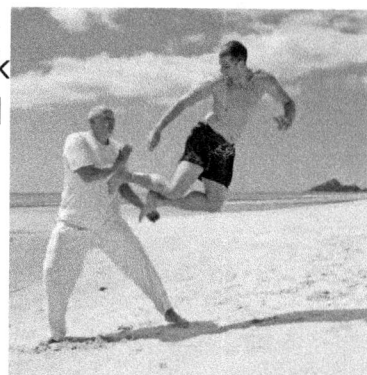

The 'one-two' Double Flying Back Kick Combo

Description

The Illustrations show how the kick is *preferably* delivered *after at least one full step for momentum-building.* You then lift the rear knee high and jump up into the forward spinning move. This is all just as if executing the simple Flying Back Kick. As soon as the Flying Back Kick has connected, you use the other leg to deliver a second Back Kick, *instead of going down for landing.* You will land on the foot that has delivered the first kick. You can kick at two different levels (high, then low), or at the same level, as the circumstances dictate.

The surprising and surprisingly easy Double Flying Back Kick

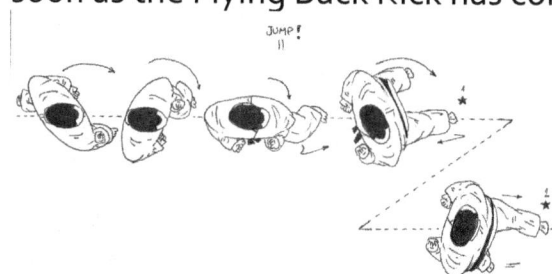

Top view of this Double Flying Kick Combination

Key points

- As you have to stay airborne longer, the *momentum of the jump* is important.
- You must use an *airborne twist* of the hips to switch from the first kick to the second. Make sure it is not a continuation of the starting spinning motion, as your momentum must be exclusively straight forward.

Targets

All targets on the head and body. The second kick can also target the groin.

Typical Application

The Drawings show an unconventional use of the Kick without a "running" step, but this time as a *timed Stop Kick*. The jump up is in fact an evasion from a classical front leg Sweep attack, that you know is coming after a lunging Reverse Punch. The first kick of the combo will connect with the opponent still moving forward, and the second will finish him up.

Jump off both feet to avoid a Sweep and stop-kick the opponent with the Double Flying Back Kick

Specific training

- The kick must be practiced on a *marked heavy bag*. Begin by executing it as a Running Kick, preceded by at least two full steps. This will help you learn to regulate the length of your steps according to the gap to cover.
- Prepare your drill by practicing the Essential *grounded* Spin-forward Back Kick. Then drill the same kick followed by another grounded Back Kick with the other leg, just as if you were preparing the flying combination on the ground. Then practice the regular Flying Back Kick. Only after all those drills, put it all together and drill the Double Flying Back Kick Combination.

Self defense

As a single kick, it is a great kick **to break an encirclement** in a real self-defense situation, or to overpower and then **overtake** an assailant in order to leave the scene and disappear (kick and keep moving...). It is also very useful against a **retreating** assailant. All these applications are about making use of the very strong momentum of this kicking combination.

➡️

...The last Figures of this section will then show the use of the kick in an *aggressive* combination **against a retreating opponent**. Note that your first attacks help to build the forward momentum. And please remember that part of stunning an opponent is to keep him off balance by alternating the heights and angles of attack. In the example presented, you attack with a classic *high* Reverse Punch, which pulls naturally the rear leg into a strong *Low* Soccer Kick. You follow up seamlessly with a *high* Jab/Cross Combination that pulls your rear knee into the forward-spin move. Jump-up and deliver both Back Kicks to the body (*mid-level*). As you land, immediately attack *high*, in this example with a front-leg Outside Crescent Kick which takes you back to centerline.

Gather momentum forward with a series of aggressive attacks; then deliver the Double Flying Kick

Illustrative Photos

The grounded version of this Flying Kick would be a Spin-forward Back Kick followed by a regular classic Back Kick. A good preparatory drill

25. THE FLYING ONE-AND-A-HALF SPIN-BACK BACK KICK

General

The last kick we shall present in this Part about classic 'Flying Kicks' is a bit of a stretch; I did consider omitting it on the grounds of it being over-spectacular. This is simply a front-leg Flying Back Kick, but *after a full spin-and-a-half*. This kick is an especially acrobatic kick, and in my opinion, not very practical in the sense that many other, safer and more effective options are always available. I have seen it executed in combat though, and we will therefore present the kick anyway, but in an abridged way. It could be considered a kick to practice for the general improvement of your flying- and spinning flying-kicks. It can be surprising, but you spend a long time getting to target, some of this time totally blind, and most of it fully airborne. In any case, it is an elegant way to close our list of Flying Kicks. Check this kick and try it up at least a few times.

Description

The drawings show it all: after a full step forward, you start your spin-back motion and accelerate as you lift your (formerly) front knee. You keep spinning while jumping off the last foot into *a full 360 airborne twist with chambered legs*. Once you are again with your back towards the opponent (after a full turn) you execute a **Back Kick** with what was your front leg.

The Flying One-and-a-half Spin-back Back Kick: an acrobatic affair

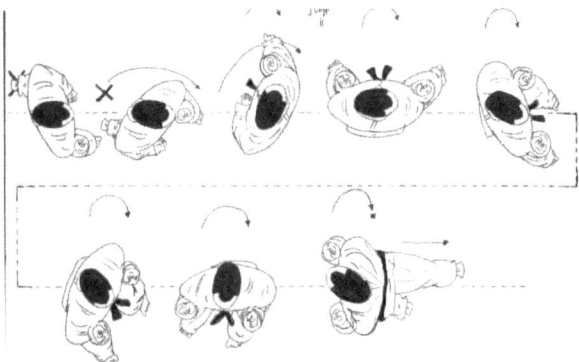

Top view of the Kick delivery

26. Plyometric Exercises

There is no escaping it: if you want to do *Flying Kicks*, you will need to be able to jump high! This is why Flying Kicks are more suited to small ectomorphic fighters than to big heavy ones.

This work does not describe general training methods in detail, as it would be too much information. In the case of Flying Kicks, it is important though, as only good jumping skills and a minimum of air-time control will allow for any ability. Someone wanting to become proficient at Flying Kicks or even to improve his jumping skills will need a lot of training. The most important exercises for proficiency in high jumps and in Flying Kicks are the **Plyometrics** [The author shamelessly recommends another of his works to the reader interested in bettering the explosiveness of all his kicks, including his Flying Kicks: *Plyo-Flex Training for Explosive Martial Arts Kicks*].

Plyometric Drills are used to increase the speed and power of muscular contractions and to provide explosiveness for many sport applications. The purpose of Plyometrics is to improve speed-based power, as required, among others, for high jumping. Jump height will be determined by how fast you are moving once your legs have left the ground. It is interesting to note that good "jumpers" need not have exceptional leg strength, but they must be able to deliver power at exceptional speeds. The applications to Basketball and Martial Arts are obvious. **Plyometric Training** is based on specific movements that toughen tissues and train nerves to stimulate a very specific type of muscle contraction: *as strong a contraction as possible in the shortest amount of time*. Sport science shows that a plyometric contraction involves a rapid muscle lengthening movement (*eccentric phase*), followed by a short resting phase (*amortization phase*), then an explosive muscle shortening movement (*concentric phase*), which enables muscles to work in tandem for the particular motion.

Plyometrics are critical for jumping/flying skills, but they are also important for many other aspects of Martial Arts; *'closing the distance'* comes to mind. We shall only describe a few basic drills important for ***high jumping***. Some people will tend to look down upon those as boring or simplistic-looking; they would be doing a serious mistake!

CAUTION: Plyometrics are stressing exercises and should only be practiced <u>after thorough warming up and some flexibility drills</u>! This safety aspect of these drills cannot be underlined enough, as a lot of energy is dispensed on the joints and tendons.

➤

The Drills:

a. Drill 1

See the Photos below. Start by standing with both feet on the same side of a line.

First Plyometric Drill: Minimize ground time

Keep your feet together and jump to the other side of the line without touching it. Keep jumping back and forth for as long as you can. Make sure that you jump *as fast as you can*: measure your progress by the amount of times you have jumped over the line. You can jump in place, or progress gradually forward as illustrated.

b. Drill 2

As illustrated in the Photos, repeat Drill 1 *on one foot,* as fast as possible back and forth. When exhausted, switch feet.

On one foot: hop back and forth as fast as possible

c. Drill 3

This is the classic **Burpee**, illustrated in the Photos below. Stand with your feet shoulder width apart. Squat down low enough so your hands can touch the floor on both sides of your legs and kick your legs out behind you into push-up position. Then, bring your legs back in and jump, **immediately,** as high as you can. Continue to repeat this exercise for as long as possible, *no resting between jumps.* The photos show the drill with an actual push-up; recommended but not essential.

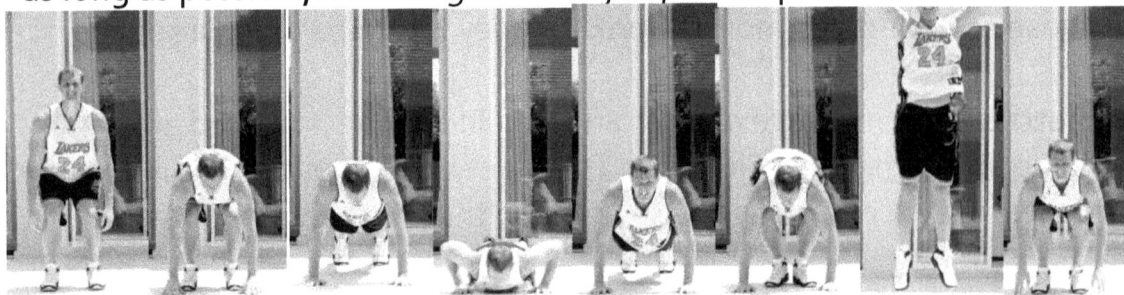

An unavoidable classic drill

d. Drill 4

Start by standing on a training box and step off, as illustrated in the Photos. **As soon as** you land, *jump as high as you can*. Repeat *immediately*. Strive to minimize the ground time between the landing and the high (*highest possible*) jump.

Classic box-off plyometric jump

e. Drill 5

On-box jumps are well-known and extremely important. The Photos show how you stand in front of a training box and jump with both feet onto it. Step down or hop down and repeat **immediately**. Keep at it for as long as possible.

Classic on-box plyometric jumps

f. Drill 6

See Photos. Drill repeatedly your **longest** possible both-feet-together **forward jump**. No rest!

Long jumps in series

27. OTHER FLYING KICKS

Here are, briefly, a few *Flying Kicks* or *Near-flying Kicks* that we have categorized and presented in other sections of previous books of the 'Kicks' series.

27.1 *Essential Kicks*

As mentioned, many *Flying Kicks* are simply extended versions of **Essential** basic Kicks of three types:

- a. Front-leg (Hopping) basic Kicks
- b. Hopping (rear-leg) Kicks
- c. Switch Kicks

For those, the reader is referred to the treatise about ***Essential Kicks***.

Front-leg Hopping Roundhouse Kick

Front-leg Hopping Side Kick

Rear-leg Hopping Roundhouse Kick

Rear-leg Hopping Front Kick

Switching jump

Switch Front Kick

Switch Low Straight-leg Roundhouse Kick

27.2 The Flying Stomp Side Kick to the knee

This has been classified as a **Low Kick**. You simply jump *high* to side-kick *low* onto the opponent's knee with the added power of your stomping body weight.

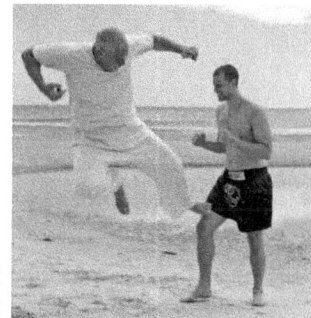

Flying low Side Kick: both a Low Kick and a Flying Kick

27.3 The Flying Stomp Kick

Also presented in our book about **Low Kicks**, this has been seen in MMA fights and is brutal. Jump *high* and *stomp* as you land! Ouch!

The no-mercy Flying Stomp

27.4 Flying Drop Kicks

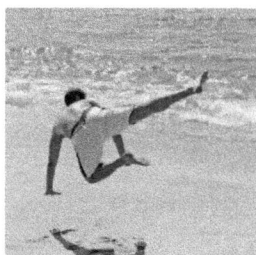

The Drop Flying Side Kick

Those are **Drop Kicks** in which you throw yourself to the ground *while* kicking; we have classified them as 'Near-suicide' Kicks for obvious reasons. See Part Two of this book.

27.5 Other Near-suicide Kicks

There are plenty of other Flying 'Near-suicide' Kicks in which one jumps to kick while soft landing is in no way assured. We shall go in more detail in the coming section. Three examples are given at the top of next page, although there are many more. *Full Suicide Kicks* per se will be presented in the next part of the book.

➡️

Suicide Twin Flying Crescent Kick to both sides of the head of the opponent

Flying Roundhouse from caught-leg position

*Somersault Downward Heel Kick: A **Kyokushinkai** favorite*

It's not the will to win that matters – everyone has that.
It's the will to prepare to win that matters.
~Paul William "Bear" Bryant

PART TWO

SUICIDE KICKS

Suicide Kicks - General

General

We have named this section and this bunch of kicks **Suicide Kicks**, again in the vein of the Sacrifice Throws (*Sutemi Waza*) of Judo, in which you sacrifice your own balance in order to throw your opponent. The difference with the previous Classic Flying Kicks is that we are now dealing with more of a sacrifice and even closer to 'suicide': <u>you know from the start that you are ending on the ground</u>; but you hope to land a serious kick on your opponent and take him down with you. Of course, this is an especially interesting tool for the good ground-fighter or the well-trained grappler. Experienced Artists and followers of MMA fighting will immediately understand that the 'suicidal' move is not that problematic. This is more a way of expressing the going voluntarily down than anything else. Readers of our previous book about **Ground Kicks** already know that being on the ground can be an extremely advantageous position. And good grapplers will love this aggressive way to go to the ground. The Kicks that we shall describe here are techniques in which you forfeit or compromise your own balance and in which you place yourself in a potentially dangerous position *in order to score*. The Suicide bit is obviously an exaggeration: everything else being equal, the effect of surprise will usually bring you victory. And even if you miss, you can always salvage your position with a few good *Ground Kicks*. The advantage of these *special Sacrifice Kicks* is that, because they are 'suicidal', they will always surprise.

We have already described kicks that could have been categorized as *Near-suicide Kicks* in previous work about more conventional kicking. For example, all the *Essential Drop Kicks*; or a special kick like the *Essential Drop Overhead Back Kick*. Those are certainly Near-suicide Kicks. We have also argued above that *Flying Kicks* are, in a way, 'Sacrifice' Kicks as well. So all this is not as far-fetched as it may sound.

The Kicks presented here will take the 'sacrifice' aspect a little bit further though, towards the suicidal, but just as a way of speaking. When you start the technique, you simply already know that your chances of landing on your feet are pretty slim. These Kicks represent a very important and interesting concept, and should be at least become familiar to all serious Martial Artists.

The advantages and disadvantages of Suicide Kicks are identical to those described in the first part of the book for regular Flying Kicks. Everything else is straightforward for the common sense-endowed reader. So let us go right to the Kicks themselves...

The Kicks

28. THE SUICIDE DROP SIDE KICK

General

This is a typical example of what we have chosen to call 'Suicide' Kicks, although the "sacrifice" aspect of the kick is a question of emphasis or even of state-of-mind. This Kick is in fact a *jumping variation* of the basic Essential *Drop* Side Kick. It could also be considered an early way to deliver the *Ground* Side Kick (See 'Ground Kicks'). It could be even looked upon as a low altitude variation of the *Flying* Side Kick, as presented in the previous part of this book. The reader is again invited to understand that there are an infinite number of variations in between all those possible kicks, and that the right version must be used according to the circumstances and to the state of mind at the time. The way to look at different kicks is also highly subjective; this is why Basic Kicks should be drilled thoroughly and then adapted to your own preferences.

The **Suicide Drop Side Kick** is basically a basic Drop Side Kick in which you have no time to drop down on your knee and hands; you therefore jump in the air directly in chambered position and kick while you receive yourself on your hands. Once you have surmounted your fear of falling, this is a fantastic kick. It can be easily used as a surprising Stop Kick. It can also be used as a counter, or even sometimes offensively.

Suicide Drop Side Kick- Dotan De Bremaeker

Description

From your guard position (preferably more of a 'sideway stance' and with more weight on your rear leg), you let yourself fall down while jumping from both feet directly into "Flying Side Kick Chamber" position. You kick while catching yourself on your hand(s), in order to break and slow the fall. Chamber back the kicking leg as you fully land on your side, but in ground guard and ready to keep kicking. See Drawings. ➤

The Suicide Drop Side Kick – Front View

The Suicide Drop Side Kick – Side View

Key points

- There should be *no telegraphing*: fall directly into airborne chamber position.
- Ideally, your kick should *connect as your hands get to the floor* for maximum power delivery.
- Fall in place, *never backwards*, and always with a "forward" mental bias.
- Your hands must *push back* up as they land on the floor, to brake your fall, to give you support, and to provide forward kicking momentum.

Typical Application

The Illustrations below show the classic **Stop Kick** application against a stepping Lunge Punch. As he starts his punching maneuver, fall down on your hands with a forward bias while stop-kicking him in the lower abdomen. Follow up with further *Ground Kicks*.

Suicide Drop Side Stop Kick against a classic Lunge Punch

Specific training

- Practice the kick on a judo mat, or on a sandy beach, for *confidence building*.
- Work on the *heavy bag*, from different ranges.
- Work on a *swinging* heavy bag (thrown by a partner) for timing, speed and stopping power.

Drill the Suicide Drop Side kick on the beach to build confidence

Self defense

The first example shows the applied kick against a roundhouse-kicking opponent. After retreating a few times, you have convinced your opponent that you are a "fleer". He will be emboldened to kick longer and further in order to 'catch' you. But you stop-kick him with the Suicide Drop Side Kick, preferably in the groin. Follow up. In this example, you twist as you land into the preparatory position for a powerful Ground Twin Back Kick (See *Ground Kicks*).

The groin Suicide Drop Side Stop Kick against a high Roundhouse

The application below shows the use of the maneuver against a rushing or a 'crowding' assailant. In the example, the opponent wields a blunt weapon and suddenly rushes to attack you. You just have time to let yourself fall down in place, while kicking. But his momentum will cause him to impale his throat on your foot blade. Follow up from the ground, for example with a Scissor Kick to his leg.

When overwhelmed suddenly, dive to the ground while kicking; aim for the throat

The last example will be 'kind of' an offensive version *against a counter puncher*: you simply won't be there for the counter. Fake a long committed jab and retreat as soon as the expected counterpunch is on the way. Dive down in place to catch him with your Suicide Side Stop Kick. As soon as you land, you can follow up with a Ground Roundhouse Kick powered by a full hip twist.

Suicide Side Stop Kick against a provoked Reverse Counter Punch

Good, better, best. Never let it rest. 'Til your good is better and your better is best.
~St. Jerome

29. THE SUICIDE DROP FRONT KICK

General

This kick is also a rather typical Suicide Kick, although very different in principle from the previous Suicide Drop Side Kick. The Suicide Front Drop Kick is basically a "fall-on-your-backside-while-kicking" maneuver. Before practicing it, refer to its close relatives: the classic *Drop Front Kick* (Essential Kicks) in which you get to the ground *then* kick; and the *Ground Front Kick* (Ground Kicks) executed if being *already* on the ground. Of course, the boundaries between these versions are very wide and blurry: the kick can be executed as a hybrid of different types, according to the circumstances. In the classic Suicide Drop Front Kick, you let yourself drop to the floor more vigorously than with the Essential Drop Front Kick, *all the while attempting to start kicking while you are dropping*. The kick can be delivered as a single or as a twin kick, and in several different ways that we will present here. This is an easy kick to deliver and it is very versatile, but you have to get familiar with the **drop** first. The drop itself is basically a Rear Judo Break-fall (*Ushiro Ukemi*), executed in a more acrobatic way.

Description

The classic way to execute the kick is presented in the Illustrations below, and at the top of next page, for both the *single* kick and the *twin* kick versions. The twin version is presented only as a reference because it is relevant to the rearwards roll; it will be presented separately in the next section. The principle is pretty simple: you fall backwards in a classic *Judo* Rear Roll fall-break, and you extend the legs in a front kick while rolling. Once you become proficient, you will start to throw yourself rearwards more vigorously into the roll *while kicking*, for a faster and more explosive kick. Once mastered, this is a surprising and very effective technique.

The Suicide Drop Front Kick

The Suicide Drop Twin Front Kick: both legs kick simultaneously

Key points

- Kick as *early* as possible in your fall.
- Place your *chin on your chest* to protect your head while falling.
- The kick is a regular *full Front Kick*, with the hip push, the chamber and the chamber-back.

Typical Applications

The Figures below show the application of the kick against a full powered Hook Punch. In our example, you have noticed the tendency of your opponent to jab/hook his openings; so you block the Jab and dive down below the Hook's arc. Catch him with the Suicide Kick in the groin or plexus as he is driven by his forward momentum. Follow up.

Evade a high Hook by falling down into the kick

The Drawings at the top of next page illustrate a typical *teaching* combination with a whole family of variations of the kick and ultimately capped with the very dangerous *Pull-in Ground Front Kick* (Refer to 'Ground Kicks'). Against a classic stepping Lunge Punch, you will evade 'in' while executing a traditional simultaneous High Outside Block/Reverse Punch. The Block turns into a catch of the punching wrist while you 'sit' down. Kick his inside thigh while rolling/falling back. Keep hold of his caught wrist. Immediately switch legs to kick his groin. Switch legs again for a Pull-in Upward Ground Front Kick to the chin. (**Careful in training, this is an extremely dangerous technique**).

➡

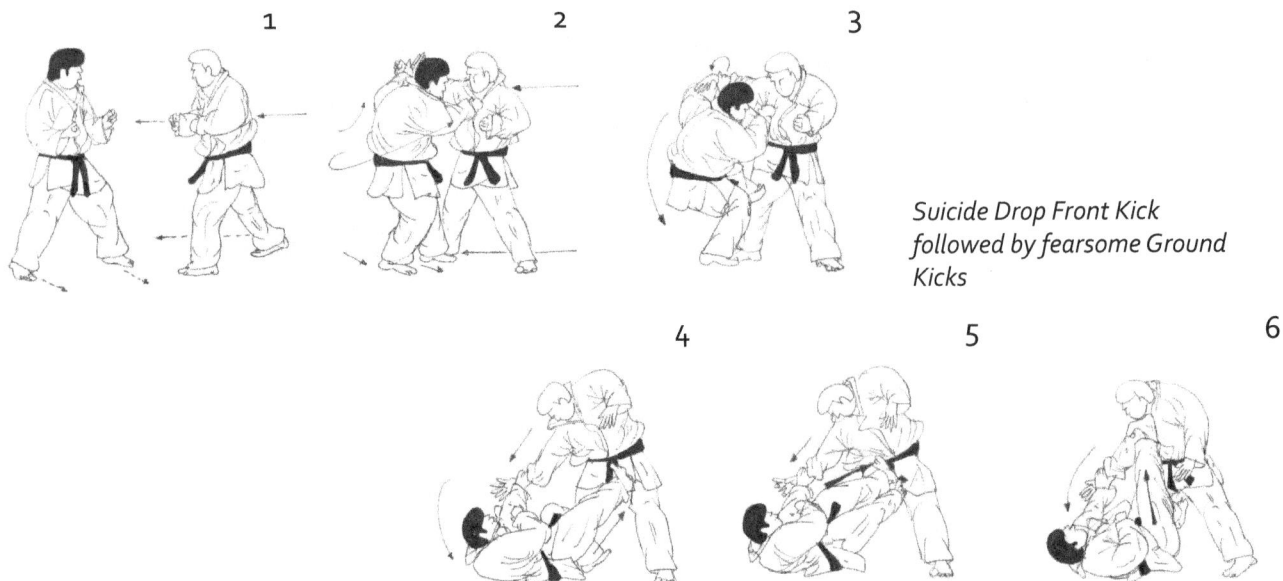

Suicide Drop Front Kick followed by fearsome Ground Kicks

Specific training

- Practice the Judo back roll (*Ushiro Ukemi*): strong, fast and jumping airborne.
- Practice the Kick while concentrating on trying to kick *as early as possible* in the roll.
- Drill on the hanging *heavy bag*. Mark the bag for precision target proficiency.

Targets

Solar Plexus, groin, thighs, knees, shins. Preferably the groin though.

Self defense

Our example, illustrated at the top of next page, describes a *very different* execution for use from a further distance. Basically it will be a <u>Dynamic</u> *Ground Front Kick* delivered from a position in which you arrived after a forward front roll; said front roll having being used only to close the distance. You'll extend the leg into the kick *as you land* from your energetic distance-closing Front Roll. This is *not* to be confused with the Forward Roll Kick presented later in the book, and which mechanics are very different {The Forward Roll Kick is a downward kick used for shorter ranges}

➡️

In this very traditional example, your assailant comes from afar and wields a long staff (*Bo*), but it could as well be a baseball bat or a chair. As he launches a high horizontal or diagonal strike to your head, you roll forward to avoid the strike, while adjusting your roll to the distance to cover. At the end of the roll you find yourself on your back in front of him, *just as if you had dropped in the classic Back Roll presented before*. You should kick **as early as possible** towards his groin, in a classic Penetrating forward Front Kick motion; *you do not kick downwards*. Aim for the groin and follow up. Do not look at this technique at a primary level, i.e. use it if you are attacked with a long staff...Drilling this series is excellent for situational kicking proficiency: it will condition your body and mind to intuitively kick from any position or motion.

The same Kick but getting into position forwards and from further away

And finally, the Illustrations below bring us back to show the *classic Ushiro Ukemi version* against a short stick strike. "Sit" to avoid the attack, groin-kick early, follow-up by twisting first into the powerful Ground Side Kick chamber. Drill this example by falling explosively and fearlessly. Simple and efficient!

The drop is best used as an evasion from a high strike; in this case, a stick attack

30. THE SUICIDE DROP TWIN FRONT KICK

General

This kick has been described in the previous section, together with the *single* version for reason of clear illustration. The two Kicks are similar during most of their execution. The reader is also invited to refer to the *Essential* Twin Drop Front Kick and the Twin *Ground* Front Kick presented in previous work. In the Suicide Drop Twin Front Kick, you basically drop down powerfully into a Back Roll and kick with both feet as early as possible in the dive. All the relevant information having been already presented, we shall just add here an additional typical application.

Typical Application

All applications presented for the previous Suicide Kick, as well as those of the related Essential and Ground Kicks, are relevant to the use of this Twin Kick. A Twin Kick is sometimes a preferable option because it 'gives it all' and the symmetry of development allows for a more powerful delivery; this is especially noticeable if used as a Stop Kick. It still stays a rather anecdotic kick, but good to drill for overall proficiency. We shall therefore present a slight variation of the Kick. As clearly apparent in the Illustrations below, this version emphasizes the hip push by lifting the whole body on the neck and shoulders during the kick. You can even, if possible, try to grab the opponent's ankle if in range for further anchoring. The application shown is a counter to a powerful push which you do not resist. You either know your opponent or have read his intentions. You go with the push and dive down to roll back. As soon as you roll onto your shoulders you twin-kick towards his chin while lifting the hips. If you have caught his ankle with one hand, all the better. Follow up with Ground Kicks, for example a Scissor Kick to his front leg.

A variation of the Suicide Drop Twin Front Kick against a violent push

31. THE KNEE-DROP SIDE KICK

General

This is a Side Kick to the knee delivered *while getting down on the knee* of the standing leg. This is a Stop Kick I have encountered in both *Korean Hapkido* and in *Vietnamese Viet Vo Dao*. It is somewhat exotic and quite difficult to execute, but it could be interesting for the adept ground fighter. I should add that I am not a big fan of the kick; it is not very healthy for the knee joint and I do not think it very practical. Proficiency also requires a lot of training, for what is a minor variation. But we need to be complete and its drilling can be interesting for some, especially as a surprise move.

Description and application

The Kick is in fact a Ground- or a Drop- Side Kick, executed as early as possible in the development. In fact, this the way that proficiency is acquired, as we shall describe in the specific training section. The end result is illustrated below: you chamber a front-leg Side Kick and start delivering it at knee level while going down on your rear knee. It is a *Stop Kick*, starting as your opponent initiates his move forward; it therefore requires good timing and a strong follow-up.

The applied Knee Drop Side Stop Kick

Specific training

- The way to start practicing the kick is presented in the Illustrations at the top of next page; going through all stages also helps understand the logic of the move. It is recommended to drill the regular standing in-place front-leg Side Kick first and the regular Ground Side Kick. Once the principles of the Side Kick are acquired, you can go gradually through the following series: First you drop into a classic Ground Side Kick *with hands and knee on floor*; it is in fact an Essential Drop Side Kick {**Stage 1**}. Try to kick early, before the hands touch the floor. You can then proceed to kneeling on your rear knee *before* kicking {**Stage 2**}. Once it is going smoothly, you can start increasing speed and try to kick earlier and earlier in the maneuver. You'll finally be able to kick with the front leg *while dropping* on your rear knee {**Stage 3**}. ➡

...

- *Protect* the knee while going down by using a thick knee pad or by working on a mat or in the sand.
- Work with a *protected partner* for the timing part of this stop-kick.

Phase 1

Phase 2

Phase 3

Self defense

The principles behind this Stop Kick are clear and it can be used wherever you feel comfortable. A good use would be as a *Cutting* Stop Kick against a high kicking attack; i.e. kicking the standing leg of the kicker. Follow up immediately with a flurry of Ground Kicks.

The Knee-drop Suicide Cutting Stop Kick against high kicker

32.   THE SUICIDE SPIN-BACK HOOK KICK

General

This is relatively safe and very efficient Kick: it is a forward-going version of the Drop Spin-back Downward Hook Kick (See *Essential Book of Martial Arts Kicks*), where the drop is executed fast. The Drop is also akin to something between a Forward and a Side Roll. In fact, a good way to describe it could be as a hybrid of the Essential Drop Kick and the Forward Roll (Mae Ukemi – Judo). You fall/roll fast to the ground, as long or as short as the situation warrants, and you use the spin to power the Kick.
The reader is referred to the above-mentioned book, as well as our work about *'Ground Kicks'*, for further reference to the close cousins of this Suicide version.
This Kick is relatively easy to execute if you have good timing. Of course, it needs serious training, but it is also fun to drill.

Description

Pictures are worth a thousand words. The series of Photos below illustrate the Kick executed in place: you twist down and roll on your shoulder to execute a Drop Spin-back Hook Kick. The kick will necessarily turn into a downward version because of your momentum.

The short version of the Suicide Spin-back Hook Kick

Typical Application

The real meaning of this kick is best understood *in context*. It is very well suited to be a *Stop Kick*, but can be also used **offensively** after causing a reaction on purpose. ➤

... In the example presented below, you jab towards the face of an established "Roundhouse-counter-attacker". As he starts to develop his counter-kick, you drop to the floor sideways on your shoulder in a typical Judo Forward Side Roll. The length of the fall/drop/jump depends on the range: It can be long or very short ("in-place"). You then use the side-and-forward rolling spin to deliver a Hook Kick to his uncovered groin. Follow up with *Ground Kicks*.

Suicide Drop Spin-back Hook Kick against provoked Roundhouse

Key points

- The Kick is delivered with the whole body, using the *momentum* of the roll.
- The Kick can only be delivered in full *commitment*.
- The *speed* of the drop and the good *distance* control are the keys to the success of the technique.
- Connect with the *heel*.
- Kick *through*, using the body to power the Kick.

Specific training

- Drill the underlying *Essential* Kicks first: the basic standing Spin-back Hook Kick, the Drop Spin-back Hook Kick, the Drop Spin-back Downward Hook Kick and the Ground Spin-back Hook Kick.
- Practice *Mae-Ukemi* in its short "in place" form and in its long "jumping" version.
- Practice the Kick, short-range and long-range, from different starting positions, using a *kick-through target* like a focus pad or a ball.

Short Front Roll

Long Front Roll

Drill the kick by kicking a ball hold by a partner

Self defense

The Figures below show that this is an ideal kick against a Downward Heel "Axe" Kick. Follow up, with a Downward Ground Roundhouse Kick for example.

Ideal against the Axe Kick; dive down fast

The photos below will show the use of the Kick as an offensive follow-up. After a powerful Roundhouse to the opponent's lower abdomen, you can lower the leg behind him while rolling to the floor into the Suicide Spin-back Hook Kick. Kick through the opponent, connecting with the heel and aiming for his groin or his solar plexus. Follow-up with *Ground Kicks*. Pay particular attention to executing this technique as a **Kick**, and **not** as a Takedown: kick *through* with focus. He will fall as a bonus. Keep kicking him...

The Suicide Drop Spin-back Hook Kick as an offensive follow-up

The Drawings below show the use of the Kick as another follow-up, but to a defensive technique. Block and catch your assailant's Jab (or initiate a front hand outside catch). You simultaneously shift to his outside and deliver an Essential Outside-tilted Heel Front Kick to his front knee. You lower the kicking leg behind him as you start the Forward Roll, and you hook-kick his solar plexus or his groin. Your other leg will go up with the Roll, most probably hooking his front leg for a bonus Scissor Takedown. As always, remember that this is a **kick** first and foremost. Follow up!

Offensive follow-up Suicide Drop Spin-back Hook Kick with takedown bonus properties

The concluding Photos below illustrate how to evade a high Roundhouse Kick by ducking, and then, to go to the ground. From there, you could execute a classic straightforward Ground Spin-back Hook Kick, or roll into a more dynamic Suicide Spin-back Hook Kick.

Go to the ground under a high Roundhouse Kick

Illustrative Photos

*The **Essential** Drop Spin-back Hook Kick*

33. THE SUICIDE ASSISTED ROUNDHOUSE FROM KNEE STOMP

General

This is an exotic technique existing in several variations in the Monkey styles of *Kung Fu* and in some *Pencak Silat* schools. It is much easier to execute than it looks and it is both very fast and very effective. The principle behind the technique is that you use the opponent's knee to support yourself while delivering a somewhat-flying Roundhouse Kick to the head (This kind of maneuver will remind the readers of 'Ground Kicks' of the **Assisted** version of Ground Kicks).

As it is a relatively complex technique to describe, we shall directly present the applications.

As a general comment, I wish to add that, after a successful Stomp Kick, there are many easier, more practical and more effective techniques to follow up with: regular kicks, punches, elbow strikes, chokes and grappling moves. But flourish with a *Suicide Kick* such as this one could be the chosen way for some...

Typical Application

The Illustrations below show the execution 'Kung Fu style', after blocking a Penetrating Front Kick. You evade the Front Kick rearwards, but slightly on the out-side; and you divert it with an Inverse Downward Block (*Gyacku Gedan Barai – Karatedo*). With your rear leg, you then deliver a 'hooking' Outside-tilted Front Kick to the back of his front knee to buckle his leg. It is a **Kick,** *not* an Assist! As soon as he starts going down, you launch a high Roundhouse Kick with the other leg, aiming for the back of his head. You go down with him, but his buckling leg is softening your fall. Land on your hands, and follow up with Ground Kicks.

Block a Front Kick to set up the Suicide Assisted Roundhouse from Knee Stomp

Key points

- Consider this kick a *Flying* Kick and execute it as such.
- Speed and power come from the airborne *body twist*. Kick 'with your hips'.
- Kick *through*. There is no hesitation and no going back. It is a fully committed kick.
- The kick to the knee "*hooks*" forward and to his in-side.

Specific training

- Drill first the regular *scissoring* Flying Roundhouse Kick presented earlier in the book, but let yourself land on the floor.
- Practice the kick on the hanging heavy bag, with a lying heavy bag on the floor for the "stomping" part of the technique.

Use two bags to drill the Suicide Kick

Self defense

The general idea of this Kick is that it can come any time you succeed in executing a Stomping Kick to the knee of the adversary. The Illustrations below show a 'Silat type' variant starting from a classic full Stomp. Evade a full-step Lunge Punch (*Oie Tsuki – Karate*) out and forward, while getting control of the punching arm. Pivot behind the assailant to stomp the back of his knee with a rear-leg Outward-tilted stomping Front Kick. As soon as he starts buckling down, jump into the Roundhouse Kick to the back of his head and land on your hands. Your other foot stays on the opponent's knee joint as he crumbles forward.

Suicide Roundhouse Kick after successful classic Knee Stomp

*A classic curving Outside-tilted Front Stomp Kick (extracted from '**Low Kicks'**)*

Success is walking from failure to failure with no loss of enthusiasm.
~Winston Churchill

34. THE SOMERSAULT DOWNWARD BACK HEEL KICK

Compasso/ Compass Pulado (Capoeira)

General

This is a family of kicks very typical of *Capoeira*, but also found in some hard Karate styles like *Kyokushinkai*. It is acrobatic, but very powerful, surprising and effective. There are many ways to practice the Kick: two-hands on floor, one–hand on floor, no hands on floor, and many variations; but we shall present only the most commonly used. These kicks are surprisingly easy to execute and to succeed with. They are very common in *Kyokushinkai* full-contact tournaments and score beautiful KO's.
Being very typical techniques, we shall present them as such, and not within application patterns. The experienced reader will have no problem is finding the optimal set-ups that suit his experience and affinities.

Description

The simplest basic version of this kick has been presented in our book about *Essential Kicks*, as the **Overhead Back Kick**. See photos below as a reminder. It is basically the 'two-hands-on-floor' version, that you should start working on first. Once you feel comfortable with it, you should start to emphasize a 'downward heel' finish with the second leg lifted.
The next logical stage is to deliver the same kick, but this time, while letting yourself fall onto your opponent after having kicked him. This allows you to place more momentum in the kick from the start onwards, and it also allows you to kick *through*. Roll into a classic Breakfall Roll of course, and always follow up on the ground with appropriate *Ground Kicks*.

The classic Overhead Back Kick

Applied Essential Overhead Back Kick with extra forward momentum

The next stage, presented in the Illustrations below, is the same exercise executed with *only one hand on the floor*. It is the classic 'Compasso' of **Capoeira**, executed totally as a *front-facing somersault*. Although delivered differently by *Capoeiristas*, you could consider this Kick an exaggerated Front Roll (*Mae Ukemi*) done on the extended arm. It could even be considered a one-hand front somersault *with some hip twist*. In any case, in order for the kick to be effective, you must emphasize the straight-leg long trajectory as a Downward Heel Kick (*Axe Kick*), even if slightly diagonal.

The one-hand Somersault Downward Back Heel Kick

The last stage of the progression would be the **no-hands** kick: It is the 'Compasso pulado' of **Capoeira** and the iconic *Do Mawashi Kaiten Geri* of **Kyokushinkai**. It is basically a front roll executed as high as possible and with an airborne twist in order to allow kicking with what becomes the rear leg. In fact, the way it is taught in *Kyokushinkai Karate* is to start as a Spin-back Hook Kick; in mid-trajectory one then jumps up while turning the kicking motion into a Diagonal Downward Heel Kick. Images are worth a thousand words: See below and in the 'Specific Training' section.

No-hands Somersault Downward Back Heel Kick; it could also be named a Flying Spin-back Diagonal Downward Hook Kick

Specific training

- Start practicing the kick on a *Judo mat* first. You must not let the fear of falling lead you to a non-committed or a non-technical Kick. Drilling on the beach is also a good confidence-builder...

...

- Drill the kick with a *partner* holding a padded target: it will make you understand that connecting with the kick always amortizes the fall. The figures below illustrate the kick in its very "*Kyokushinkai*" version: Basically starting with a Spin-back Hook Kick and then jumping and letting yourself fall with a diagonal Axe Kick.
- Only when the Kick is so mastered should you start drilling on a suspended '*kick-through*' target.
- Practice the Front Roll (*Mae Ukemi*) over a *high obstacle* or a bent-over partner.

'High' Front Roll Break-fall

Drilling the Kick on a body shield

Illustrative Photos

The Overhead Back Kick against a Spin-back Outside Crescent Kick – most appropriate

The Overhead Back Kick against a high Reverse Punch

35. THE ROLLING-FORWARD DOWNWARD KICK

General

This is the less acrobatic version of the 'Forward Roll' Kick. It is easy to execute and still very effective: you go down into the classic Forward Roll, by placing the hand and then the shoulder on the floor before starting to roll. No twists and no flying! Sometimes called the **Rolling Hill Kick**, it is a great maneuver, especially useful as a *Surprise Kick*, a *Stop Kick*, a *Going-to-the-floor Kick* or a *Distance-closer* (to reduce the range **while** kicking). It takes some work to be able to execute it as a **Kick** and not as a Roll; though it is mostly a mental adjustment coming with practice.

Description

The Illustrations below show clearly that the Kick is simply a classic *Judo* Forward Roll (*Mae Ukemi*). You just have to make sure that the kicking leg is extended at apex and gathers as much momentum as possible when going down. Connect with the heel and kick *through* the target. There are two ways to practice the Kick: (i) directly down from the standing guard position, and (ii) after a step to gather momentum. The stepping version is obviously more powerful but telegraphs an attack. **The no-step version needs to be drilled first though,** because it is the way to learn to develop the inherent power of the Kick (with no help from the momentum).

The no-step Rolling-forward Downward Kick

The stepping 'Rolling Hill' Kick

Key points

- Use the full body *momentum* into the kicking leg. This is a fully committed kick.
- Kick *through* the target: do not start bending the leg as you connect.
- Always *follow up*.
- You must mentally concentrate on the maneuver being a *Kick*, and not a Roll. Fighting is as much of the mind as of the body.

Typical Application

The most typical application of the Kick is the one using the 'bending-forward-into-the-Roll' as an evasion from a high attack, whether a high kick or a high punch. The Figures below show how you bend to evade a high Reverse Punch to the head, and then roll into the attacker, heel-kicking him and sending him down to the floor. It will then be easy to keep downward-heel-kicking him on the floor (See *Ground Kicks*).

Very natural Rolling-forward Downward Kick against a committed high Reverse Punch

Specific training

- *Mae-Ukemi* with focus and concentration.
- Kick the *hanging* heavy bag, or a hanging target, or a focus pad held by a partner.
- Kick a *heavy bag lying on the floor* to drill kicking through at maximum power. An old-fashioned 'Bean Bag Seat', if you have still one from its Seventies heyday, is a fantastic training aid.

Drill the kick-thru of the kick with a hanging focus pad

Drill the kick with no slowing until you wham a bean bag or a lying punching bag

Targets

Anything you can kick downwards from above! As illustrated above, the face. But especially surprising and painful can be the head of a bent-over opponent, or the top of his foot.

Kicking the back of the head of a bent-over opponent

Surprise: aim for the toes or the top of the foot of your unsuspecting adversary; **then** *follow up*

Self defense

Another great use of the Kick is to close the distance safely and surprisingly, after having pushed the opponent away. The Illustrations below show how you have stop-kicked an assailant with a *Pushing Front Kick*. As he stumbles away, you jump into a roll to close the range quickly. You can so surprise him with the **Rolling Downward Heel Kick,** as he has not yet digested the Front Stop Kick. Make sure to jump far into the roll (close to him), in order to compensate for the ever-increasing distance as he stumbles back to recover both his balance and his confidence. Keep kicking from the floor, as detailed in *Ground Kicks*.

The Rolling-forward Downward Kick is a great move to close the range with an opponent you have just pushed away

Illustrative Photos

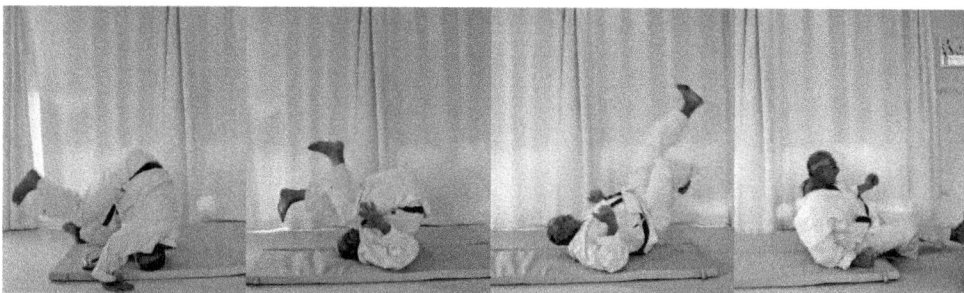

Rolling into the Downward Heel Kick

36. The Rolling-forward Downward Heel to Roundhouse Kick
and to other Follow-ups

General

This is not a kick per se, but an important maneuver to practice, as an automatic way-out in case your regular Rolling-forward Downward Heel Kick falls short and/or misses the opponent. The purpose of drilling this new 'Kick' is to ingrain a 'fallback' follow-up of sorts. The drawback of all those Suicide Kicks based on Forward Rolls of all types, is that you will not be able to know if you have correctly gauged distance and your opponent's reaction until you have completed the Roll. Should you miss, you have to be able to keep the offensive!

We shall present a few examples of these kicking maneuvers as a full 'Typical Applications'. We will present a few alternative ways to follow up after a "missed" Rolling Forward Kick. The experienced reader will take it from here and develop his own follow-ups. There are basically two ways to correct a missed Rolling Hill Kick: (i) stop and execute a Ground Kick or (ii) keep the momentum in order to stand up and follow through. Referring to the second option, any beginning Judo practitioner, will easily grasp how easy it is to stand back up after a *Mae Ukemi* (Forward Breakfall, Front Roll). Using the momentum to power a subsequent technique is the easy, and important, next step.

Typical Applications

The first example is a *Rebounding* Ground Kick after landing too short. The Illustrations below show how you initiate a rear-leg mid-level Stop Roundhouse Kick against a threatening opponent. Your opponent stumbles and retreats. You then lower the kicking leg and seamlessly roll forward, attempting a *Rolling Downward Heel Kick*. But he retreats faster than expected and you just miss him. As you land, twist immediately to deliver a **Ground Roundhouse Kick** to his groin. Follow up.

Stop on the floor after a missed Rolling Hill Kick and immediately let the leg rebound in a groin Ground Roundhouse Kick

The second example is the drill of a 'Roll-and-stand-up' variation. You roll down and stand back up in the same move, and you use the momentum of the Roll to power a subsequent Kick. This kind of maneuver has the additional effect of baffling the opponent with a change of plane and a difficult-to-gauge closing of the distance. This is very typical of *Nin Jitsu* styles, sneaky and unexpected. The standing-up at the end of the Roll is very easy and natural; it is drilled at the beginning of all *Judo* training sessions. Drilling an exercise like the one illustrated below will make you learn to both get up in a *Zanshin* (focused) position and to use the energy of the Roll for a stronger following maneuver. Drill, drill, drill.

Aggressive Forward Roll, standing up into a powerful rear-leg Front Kick

Variations

The interested reader is invited to consult our previous book about *Ground Kicks* for more examples of possible follow-up Kicks to a short Rolling Kick: nearly any Ground Kick starting from the ground end-position of the Roll is suitable. Of course, it supposes that you are a good ground fighter and interested in staying down at the end of the incomplete *Rolling Hill Kick*. The alternative is to keep the momentum and to stand-up at the end of the Roll, as will be illustrated again further down. In the first example below though, you sit up at the end of the Roll to seamlessly achieve further unexpected range with a **Ground Jumping Side Kick**; note that it would work even better should your opponent try to counterattack after your too-short *Roll Kick*.

A Rolling Hill Kick turns smoothly into a one-hand Jumping Ground Side Kick

Of course the same principles stay valid for a whole array of different Kicks. The Illustrations below show the finish-up with none else than the Jumping Ground Spin-back Hook Kick. Your opponent will think you are fumbling to stand back up after missing your Suicide Kick, while you are in fact spinning into the follow-up Kick. With a bit of luck, he could even be preparing to rush you with a counter...

Rolling-forward Downward Heel Kick fades smoothly into a Ground Jumping Spin-back Hook Kick

The next example is a variation just *in-between* the two broad categories: It is a Ground Kick from the Ground end-position, but it is also half-a standing-up move that uses the momentum of the Roll. Like always, nothing is just black or white. As illustrated, you roll up into a side kneeling position from which you execute with no interruption a *second* roll leading to a groin **Twin Roundhouse Ground Kick**. A few drawings are better than a thousand words.

The next examples will all be **standing-up versions**. Of course you can either *kick* while standing up, or *stand up into guard* and follow-up with all kinds of techniques.
It must be said that one of the advantages of the Rolling-forward Kicks is that they have a strong forward momentum *and are nearly impossible to stop*. Even if your opponent retreats enough to avoid the kick or to dilute most of its power, you still have a forward momentum that you can use to smother any counterattack and to get close to him for further attacks.

...

In the first example below, you simply *stand up* in a normal fashion at the end of the Roll, but you execute a **Low Kick** while doing so (Rear-leg Low Straight-leg Roundhouse Kick). It is pretty easy, fast and surprising.

Finishing with a simple standing-up Low Kick

A better use of the momentum of the Roll is illustrated in the next application: the follow-up Kick is a *standing-up* **Spinning-back Bent-over Hook Kick**. Drill to learn to power the Spin with the preceding Roll. It is also an important drill for overall kicking proficiency.

The very powerful Rolling Hill Kick into standing-up Spin-back Hook Kick

If you go directly into the standing-up at the end of the Roll, chances are high that you'll end up in guard very close to the opponent. The follow-up need not be a kick but any adequate Martial technique will do. You should therefore drill the Roll into _Focused_ standing guard and let your martial skills take over to choose the most suitable subsequent technique.

The next sequence, illustrated at the top of next page, shows such a situation in which you have fallen short but can smother any reaction/counter as you roll up standing, by encircling his arm (from the outside) *and* neck thanks to the strong forward momentum. You then throw him with a *Neck Twist Takedown* (**Careful**! Dangerous technique), while still making use of the powerful momentum gathered by the Roll.

➡

Roll directly into strong forward stand-up and use the energy for a dangerous Neck Twist Takedown

The Illustrations below show another technique using the powerful momentum of the full Body Roll: this time you *smash into him* while classically standing up. By doing so you smother his guard or/and any attempt to stop-punch; you can then catch and lift his front leg. Note that his retreating from your Roll will always cause a 'weightless' front leg. You can now push him back, preferably at throat level, while keeping lifting his leg; and then, reap his standing leg from under him (Hard version of *O Uchi Gari* – *Judo*). Note that this is a hard fall for the opponent and that extreme **caution** is warranted in training. Follow up.

Catch the opponent's leg while powerfully standing up from the Roll and execute a dangerous takedown

And we shall conclude this section with a flourish, especially suited against a 'Runner' (a fleeing/retreating type of opponent). The Drawings are presented at the top of next page. This may seem a little over-showy or unnecessary, but, if you are into *Suicide Kicks* or particularly like this specific one, it is a strong technique with a high chance of success. It has high chances of scoring against a systematically retreating adversary, or if you have already conditioned him to a 'too short' Rolling Hill Kick of yours. What would be more surprising than an 'encore'? After a fully-fledged *Rolling Kick* that your opponent evades by stepping back, you use the momentum to stand up **and plunge forward for an additional Rolling Kick.** You can *dive long* for the second Rolling Kick as you are still carried by the momentum of the previous one. The second, longer, Rolling-forward Downward Heel Kick has many chances of connecting: it is very difficult to 'run' rearwards faster than diving forwards!

➡

The unexpected **Double** Rolling-forward Downward Heel Kick combination

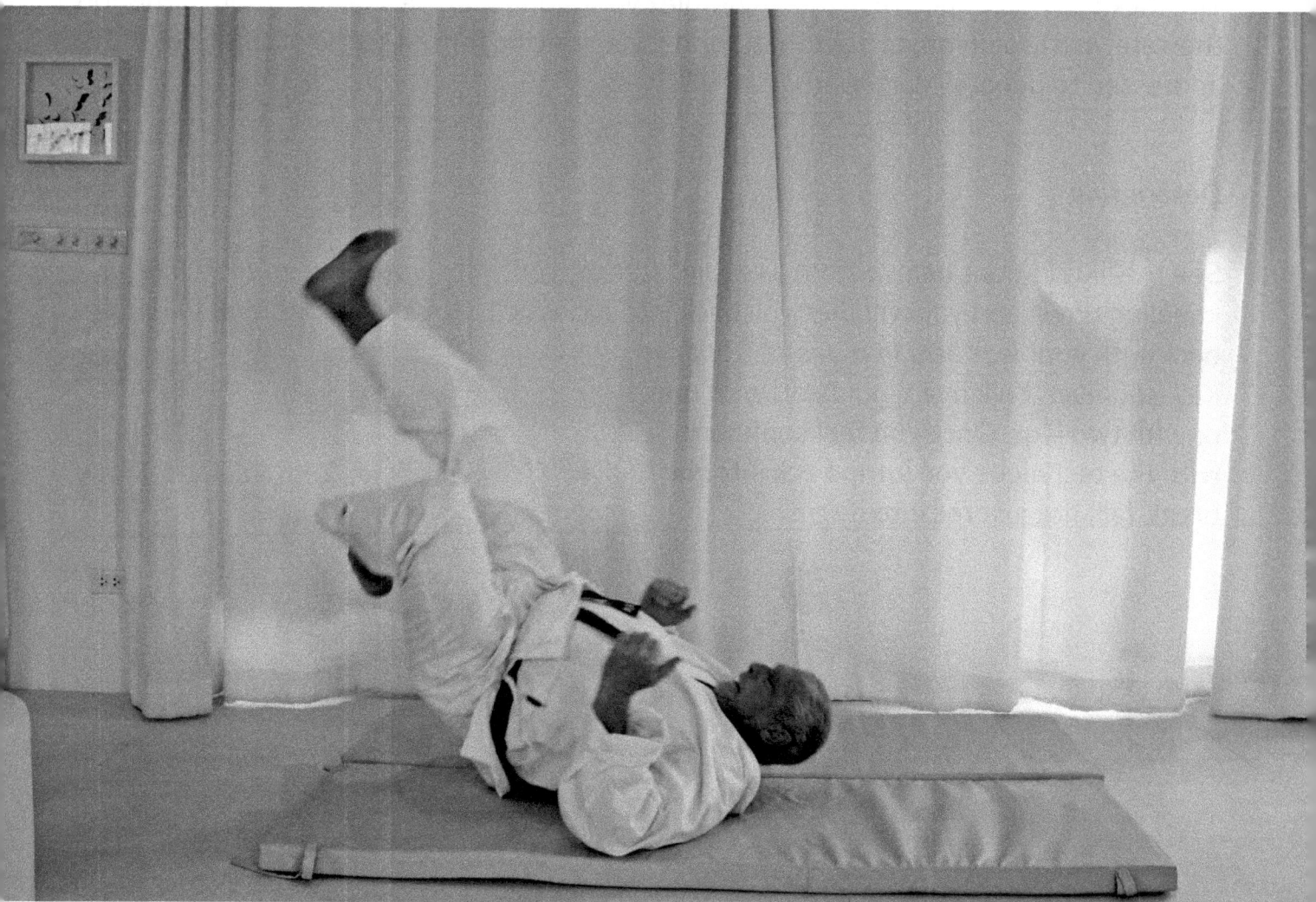

THE ROLLING-FORWARD DOWNWARD HEEL TO ROUNDHOUSE KICK

37. THE ROLLING-BACK FRONT KICK

General

We named this Kick a "Front Kick" because of the way the leg develops during the kick itself. To be accurate, it should be called a "Back" Kick because it is connecting behind you. In any case, it should be deemed even more of a 'Suicide' Kick than previous examples, because you simply turn your back to the opponent before even going down and starting the Kick. It is still surprisingly efficient though.

The Kick is basically a Back Roll (*Ushiro Ukemi – Judo*) which momentum you use to kick behind you with one or two feet. If the opponent is in front of you, *you have to pivot* before you roll down, which is somewhat dangerous; hence the 'suicide' classification. On the other hand, it is generally *very unexpected* though, and it is also a very easy kick to execute.

The Kick exists in Capoeira in more complex variations that we shall mention; although they are, in my opinion, too acrobatic and style-specific for the scope of this book, addressed to general Martial artists of all styles..

Description

See the Illustrations below: from a regular stance, you will pivot 180 degrees *while* kneeling down and you will then roll back into a classic Judo rearwards break-fall. Roll back with your *legs bent in a classic Front Kick-chamber*. Kick over your head with one or with two legs. Once you feel confident with the technique you **jump** back into the break-fall, not just roll into it.

The classic Rolling Back Front Kick

The Twin version of the Rolling Back Front Kick: kicking with both legs simultaneously

The next Figures show a **Capoeira** variation called *Macaquinho* (Monkey) in which you kneel and lean both back and sideways onto your hands (and sometimes on your head also), before kicking back. It is a different technique, but the Kick develops rearwards in the same fashion. [It should be noted that in *Capoeira*, the technique is also a kick to the front while the leg is going up. The wheeling back is then an evasion with or without the 'Back Front Kick']. This version can also be executed acrobatically in a handstand variation. These are typical *advanced* Capoeira moves, very efficient and spectacular but outside the scope of this book. The interested readers are invited to consult Capoeira literature and experiment.

The acrobatic 'Monkey' version of the Rolling Back Front Kick

Key points

- *Minimize back exposure* by pivoting and going down fast and simultaneously.
- Throw yourself back from the kneeling position for added body momentum into the kick. *Jump* and adjust distance.
- Always *follow up*: you find yourself in a very dangerous relative position at the end of the kick. Refer to '*Ground Kicks*' for ground movement and techniques.

Typical Application

The series at the top of next page shows a typical use of the Kick against a skilled high puncher. By going down, you neutralize his relative strength while also doing something unexpected. In the example, you lure him in with a short Front Kick and retract the leg back in order to cause an 'expected' high punching counterattack. Block the first punch while using the momentum of the retracting leg to pivot back and go down. Roll back *under* his following punches and kick him in the midsection. Follow up by kicking him upwards under the chin, preferably getting hold of his ankles or legs to prevent his escape. Keep kicking, for example with a Ground Overhead Twin Front Kick to throw him back. Roll back to the front to stand up safely. ➡️

Rolling Back Front Kick against a high puncher, and follow-up

Specific training

- The Illustration shows drilling with a partner holding a *focus pad*. Unlike training on the hanging heavy bag (a good drill by itself), it allows to go for the "kick-through" feeling. Train from different ranges, with different Rolls.
- Practice aggressively the Judo Back Roll (*Ushiro Ukemi*) in all its variations: high, low, jumping, short and long.

Drill kicking 'through' a focus pad

Self defense

The example below shows a classic use of the Kick in a release from an attempted rear bear hug. As soon as your assailant starts hugging you, evade down and to the side while hitting him in the groin with a hammer-fist strike. Let yourself fall down on your back, while trying to get hold of his arms. Kick him in the face or higher sternum while pulling on his arms. Keep kicking, just like in the previous example. If you have been able to get hold of his wrists or sleeves, you could follow-up with the dangerous '*Gyacku Tomoe Nage*' Jiu-Jitsu Takedown (See '*Ground Kicks*').

Escaping a rear bear hug attempt by 'falling down'

38. THE FLYING ROUNDHOUSE FROM CAUGHT-LEG POSITION

General

This is an acrobatic Suicide Kick. But it is quite easy to execute, and it is not that 'suicidal': you are in a difficult and dangerous position from which your choices are limited! When your leg has been caught by your opponent for any reason, you have to react very fast as you are at his mercy: you are off balance and the opponent can easily punch you, kick you or take you down. You have to do at once anything possible to get out of this awkward situation, even if it looks 'crazy'.

The reader is referred to a similar Caught-leg Kick described in *The Essential Book of Martial Arts Kicks'* (The **One-legged Drop Back Kick**, illustrated at the end of the section). In the case of the Flying Roundhouse reaction to the leg-catch, you simply pivot in the *other* direction; you jump up and kick with your whole body. The Kick is easier to perform than it looks, as your body weight is partly carried by the opponent and the twist makes for great power. This Kick often stars in tournaments of hard styles like *Kyokushinkai Karate*.

Description

The Kick is relevant only in specific situations, and it will be described in a **Typical Application.** The Figures below illustrate how your mid-level Roundhouse Kick is caught underarm by your opponent; whether it happened on purpose (*Trap*) or *not*. As your opponent prepares to follow up, you pre-empt by **immediately** jumping off the standing leg while pivoting airborne. Jump high and deliver the Flying Roundhouse Kick to his head *with the whole momentum of the spinning body*. Kick *through* and try to land on your hands and on your kicking leg. This would be the optimal situation, although you'll probably often end up on the floor. Your caught leg should be released by now; so get in focused guard and follow up.

Flying Roundhouse Kick on a caught regular Roundhouse

Key points

- Jump as *high* as possible and already in twisting mode.
- Jump *towards him*, then kick through and down.
- *Twist* forcefully in the air to kick with the whole body.
- No need for a chamber-back: After you have kicked *through* his head, you should concentrate on trying to *land* on this same kicking leg.

Specific training

- Start by drilling the *Front Chamber to Flying Roundhouse Kick*: lift the leg in a Front Chamber and jump off into a Flying Roundhouse (with the standing leg). See the Section above: 'Flying Front- to Roundhouse Double Kick'
- Kick *through a striking pad* held by a partner. Use a lying heavy bag, a chair, a plyometric box, a stack of aerobic stairs or a leg stool **to simulate the caught leg**. Simulate the leg caught as a Front Kick **or** as a Side/Roundhouse Kick. At the beginning, it is good to have an additional partner holding you up as you jump, in order to help you build confidence and to help you concentrate on the correct technique.

Drill the Kick with one leg straight on a stool; one partner will help you stay airborne, the other will hold a focus pad

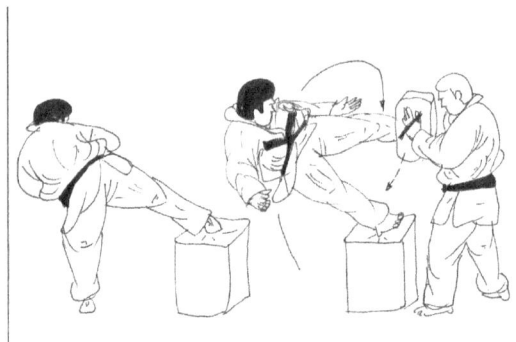

When confident, start from Side Kick position and concentrate on kicking through the pad hold by your partner

Self defense

There are not many variations on this theme: your kick gets caught or you let it get caught on purpose, and fly you go. See the example at the top of next page...

➡

...

The Figures below show the technique executed as a Front Kick of yours has been caught by your assailant on his in-side. You immediately jump off; *but, this time*, you **hook** with your ankle into his neck while completing the kick-through. By doing so, you pull him with you to the floor, using him as a brake to your descent (Be careful while practicing: ***This is a very dangerous technique***!). As soon as you land, you deliver a Ground Downward Heel Kick to his back. Keep ground-kicking.

Hooking Flying Roundhouse from a caught Front Kick; hook in while kicking through and follow up

Illustrative Photos

*The **Essential** One-legged Drop Back Kick; very similar principle*

39. THE FLYING SPIN-BACK HOOK KICK FROM CAUGHT-LEG POSITION

General

This Kick is the logical companion to the previous one: your leg is caught but you jump and pivot *in the other direction* to deliver a 'Flying' Spin-back Hook Kick. This Kick is more difficult to execute, but is also more powerful. Again it is not as difficult as it may seem because part of your body weight is held by your opponent; and landing should not be feared as it is relatively soft.

In fact, the Kick is *not* really a *classic* Hook Kick, but more of a 'Downward' version of the Hook Kick, on account of the pull of gravity. The reader is invited to refer to, and drill, the related Kicks: the Flying Spin-back Hook Kick (in this volume), the Spin-back Downward Heel Kick and the Back Kick from Caught-leg Position (both presented in the '*Essential Book of Martial Arts Kicks*')

Description

Again, the Kick is totally situational and will be described, like the previous one, in a **Typical Application**. The Figures below show how your mid-level Roundhouse Kick gets caught by the opponent in an underarm hook. Again, whether it is a mistake on your part or whether you have let yourself get caught on purpose, is irrelevant. But you **immediately** jump off the standing leg while keeping the momentum of the Roundhouse Kick. You jump *high*, you keep *pivoting* in the same direction and you *twist* forcefully while airborne into a Flying Spin-back Hook Kick to his head. Kick *through* his undefended head (as his arm is holding your leg) and reception yourself on your hands, and hopefully feet. Always follow up with other *Ground Kicks*.

The Flying Spin-back Hook Kick from Caught-leg Position

3

4

5

6

Key points

- Jump as *high* as possible and *twist* vigorously.
- This Kick can only succeed with full *commitment*: There is no holding back.
- Kick *through* the target. There is *no* stopping the momentum.

Specific training

- Drill the classic *Flying Spin-back Hook Kick.*
- Practice with a partner holding a *focus pad.* Just as for the previous kick, use a lying bag or a foot stool to simulate the caught leg.

Drilling the Kick with a partner and a stool

Self defense

Just as for the previous application presented, the Illustrations below show the use of this Suicide Kick after your regular Front Kick is encircled and caught by the opponent. But it also shows how you can kick your assailant away, if your leg is caught under his body after you both fall on the floor. If you are proficient with the Kick and a good ground-fighter, this can be a great trap in which you kick purposely to entice your opponent to catch your leg.

Front Kick caught, suicide Spin-back Hook Kick, Heel Kick to push fallen opponent away

The last Illustrations, at the top of next page, will show a slightly different scenario and a slightly different execution. This time, you start with a *Side Kick* that gets caught and with an opponent who *twists your ankle* to take you down...

...

The Downward Cross Block (*Juji Uke – Karatedo*) is a classic catch that lends itself easily to an *Ankle Twist* in the case of a Side Kick or of a Roundhouse Kick attack. If you get caught, you will have to react fast: **do not resist but go with the twist**. You then *jump* up as soon as you have your back to him. The Spin-back Flying Hook Kick in the example below turns into the Downward version, as the opponent bends over when he sees the Kick coming. You add all your weight to the momentum of the kick to crush him into the floor. Keep ground-kicking.

The Flying Spin-back Downward Hook Kick from Caught-and-twisted-leg Position

Illustrative Photos

An applied **Essential** *Spin-back Downward Hook Kick*

40. THE SUICIDE TWIN FLYING CRESCENT KICK

General

The name says it all: two Flying Inside Crescent Kicks delivered *simultaneously* to attack a target like the head *from both sides*! In its theoretical form, this Kick is unnecessarily acrobatic and dangerous. I would not have included it if I had not seen it, - with my own eyes-, executed successfully in a Kung Fu tournament. It must be said that the competitors involved were of very different levels, and the most proficient of them was making use of the situation for excessively flourishing moves. But, ultimately, the bottom line was that the Kick is effective and not so far-fetched... There is thankfully a way to deliver it in a safer and easier way, using your partner to slow your fall, by grabbing him: this will be presented as the **Application**.
The reader should refer to a corresponding **Ground Kick**, presented in previous work: the *Ground Twin Inside Crescent Kick*).

Description

The Figure shows how you jump off both feet and deliver a Twin Flying Crescent Kick: Both legs close, from outside inwards, on to the target, which is preferably the head at ear level. Break your fall. Basic training obviously includes kicking a striking pad from both sides. The Illustration also shows the top view of the Kick.

The classic execution of the Suicide Twin Flying Inside Crescent Kick

Key points

- Jump *high* with bent legs, then extend them out and close them inwards.
- *Break your fall* with a Judo Back Roll.
- *Follow up* with Ground Kicks.

Typical Application

The most practical way to deliver this Kick is in fact pretty effective: You hold your opponent as you jump, using him to soften your fall and pulling him into the Double Kick. The Illustrations below show how you initiate a high Reverse Punch in order to grab him with both hands at shoulder or upper arm level. Jump up while pulling his arms down and start delivering the Twin Crescent Kicks, aiming for his ears. At the last moment, let go of his upper limbs in order to make way for the incoming Kicks. Although you have used him to slow your own fall, roll back in a clean Rear Judo Break-fall. Follow up, with a *Ground Front Kick* to the groin for example.

1   2   3

Grab his arms to allow for a safer Suicide Kick. Always follow up

4   5   6

Specific training

- Drill high Rear Judo Rolls (*Ushiro Ukemi*)
- Practice twin-kicking a *focus pad* held by a partner. He will start holding it at groin level and lift it gradually higher.
- Practice carefully the *Typical Application* presented above, with a partner.

41. THE DROP TWIN OVERHEAD FRONT KICK

General

This is simply the twin version of the simpler Single *Rolling Back Front Kick*, previously presented. This is also a very close relative of the corresponding *Ground Kick* presented in previous work. The principles are the same and we shall just present two straightforward **Applications** for the sake of completeness.

Typical Application

The Illustrations below show the delivery of the *Twin Kick* against an opponent attacking you from behind. There is no pivot and you dive down in Back Roll as soon as you see/feel the attack coming. In this example, you get hold of your opponent's ankles for a more effective Kick. Follow up with appropriate *Ground Kicks*.

Drop Twin Overhead Front Kick with ankle catch, on an attack from behind

Key points

Refer to §37 and to the '*Ground Overhead Twin Front Kick*' (Ground Kicks).

Specific training

Refer to §37 and to the '*Ground Overhead Twin Front Kick*' (Ground Kicks).

Self defense

The Figures below show the basic version against an assailant in front of you, with a pivot and with no ankle grab. In this example, you are 'timing' a rear-leg Full Roundhouse high Kick, but the technique would be good and surprising against any similar *committed* attack. Follow up with *Ground Kicks*.

A suicidal 'timing' Drop Twin Overhead Front Stop Kick against a committed high Roundhouse

+++++++++++++++++++++++++++++++

IN MEMORIAM
SENSEI SIDNEY SHLOMO FAIGE

It is up to us to live up to the legacy that was left for us, and to leave a legacy that is worthy of our children and of future generations.
~Christine Gregoire

42. THE DROP PULL-IN LOW KICK

General

This is a Kick probably derived from the old Japanese *Ju Jitsu* styles: you deliver a *Low Front Soccer Kick* (See 'Low Kicks') to your opponent's shin while pulling him towards you and so placing his body weight on to the targeted leg. In order to maximize both kick power and pull effectiveness, you let yourself fall on your side (*Yoko Ukemi* – Judo) while doing so.

In fact, this kicking maneuver is a close relative to a Judo Side-Sacrifice Throw named *Yoko Gake* and presented in the Figures below: you place your opponent off-balance by pulling him up and forward and execute a classic sweep while letting yourself fall on your side and pulling him in. You **lift** the swept ankle as you both go down, and your opponent's fall is therefore quite hard. The *Judo* version is all about placing the opponent off-balance before the takedown (*Kuzushi*). In the non-sport version of this Sacrifice Throw, it is more about the Kick: you **kick** first instead of sweeping, and then use your fall to generate more power and get him to the ground!

The classic Judo's Yoko Gake

Description

The simplest version of this Kick is presented in the Illustrations *at the top of next page*. In this offensive application, you initiate a typical *catching move*: a high lunging Jab aimed at provoking a block and in turn at getting hold of your opponent's wrist or sleeve. It also should have your opponent starting a retreating move while getting himself slightly off-balanced. You then keep the powerful forward momentum to get hold of the opponent's shoulder (or sleeve at triceps level) with your other hand. Pull while delivering a **powerful** *Low Front Soccer Kick* to his front shin and while letting yourself fall. Kick *through* the opponent's shin and *keep lifting his leg* while pulling him to the floor: it will cause a nasty fall, difficult to control (**Caution**!). Follow up, by punching first and then ground-fighting. There are numerous possible variations to this Kick: kicking before or while falling, keeping hold of his wrist or not, starting in matching or in opposite stances, and more. The reader is invited to experiment. ➡️

An offensive Drop Pull-in Low Kick

Typical Application

The application below shows a different version of this Kick that is very common in Southern *Kung Fu* styles and in Indonesian Arts: you kick while letting yourself fall, but you brake your fall by keeping hold of the opponent's wrist, **and** you also leave your kicking foot on his shin to use as an anchor point. In the example presented, you get hold of his front wrist with a classic feint. You then kick to the opponent's knee, **hard**, while letting yourself down on your other hand. In this maneuver, you will then use your foot on his knee and your hand on the floor as anchor points for a full powered *Roundhouse Kick* to his face, in which you use the *body twist for a kick-through*. Remember to keep pulling on his caught wrist all the time. Keep using *Ground Kicks* after landing.

An applied close relative of the Drop Pull-in Low Kick

Specific training

- Practice the classic *Yoko Gake* Throw on a Judo mat.
- Practice the side fall-break (*Yoko Ukemi*) for confidence, high and hard.
- Drill the classic *grounded* Low Soccer Front Kick for *power* (Tire, heavy bag,...).

Self defense

The Figures below show an advanced version of this kicking Takedown in which you add to the throw the strong leverage of a '**hit and pull**' on the inside elbow. It makes your opponent's fall even worse than with the classic version. The applied example presented below starts with an inside forward evasion and a rear hand block against a lunge-punching assailant. You then catch his attacking wrist and *hammerfist* his elbow, while executing a strong *Drop Pull-in Low Kick*. Keep pulling *and lift your kicking foot to cause him to fall from even higher*. Follow-up.

A reinforced Drop Pull-in Kick Takedown

[**This is here the place to open a _Parenthesis_ in this "kicking" treatise and underline how effective hitting an attacking limb can be. The Illustrations below show several possible and unconventional attacks to a limb which you control with the other hand: 'Door knock' Strike to the elbow joint, Hammer-fist Strike to the inside elbow, Hammer-fist Strike to the biceps muscle, Hook Punch to the elbow joint, Upward Backfist to the elbow joint...And there are more... Of course, I urge you to follow up with a ... _Kick_!**]

Examples of attacks on a caught arm; **respectively**: *elbow door knock, biceps hammer, elbow hook, elbow hammer, elbow upward backfist*

We shall now present another variation of this *Suicide Kick*, based on another old *Jiu-Jitsu* Sacrifice Takedown. Instead of a *Soccer Low Kick*, you will attack the opponent's leg with a **Crescent Kick** while pulling him down. This technique is, again, about **kicking** first and foremost. But the best way to get the 'feel' of it before concentrating on the kicking part, is to drill two *Judo* Takedowns of the *Yoko Sutemi Waza* (Side Sacrifice Techniques). It is important to drill both, because the '**kicking**' version of the technique is less pure and will fall somewhere in between the <u>Side Pull</u> (*Yoko Otoshi*) and the <u>Front Pull</u> (*Uki Waza*), according to the circumstances and the success of the execution. Once you have mastered the *Judo* techniques, you should concentrate on the set-up, as illustrated below, **and on the 'kicking hard and through' part**.

Classic Judo's Yoko Otoshi

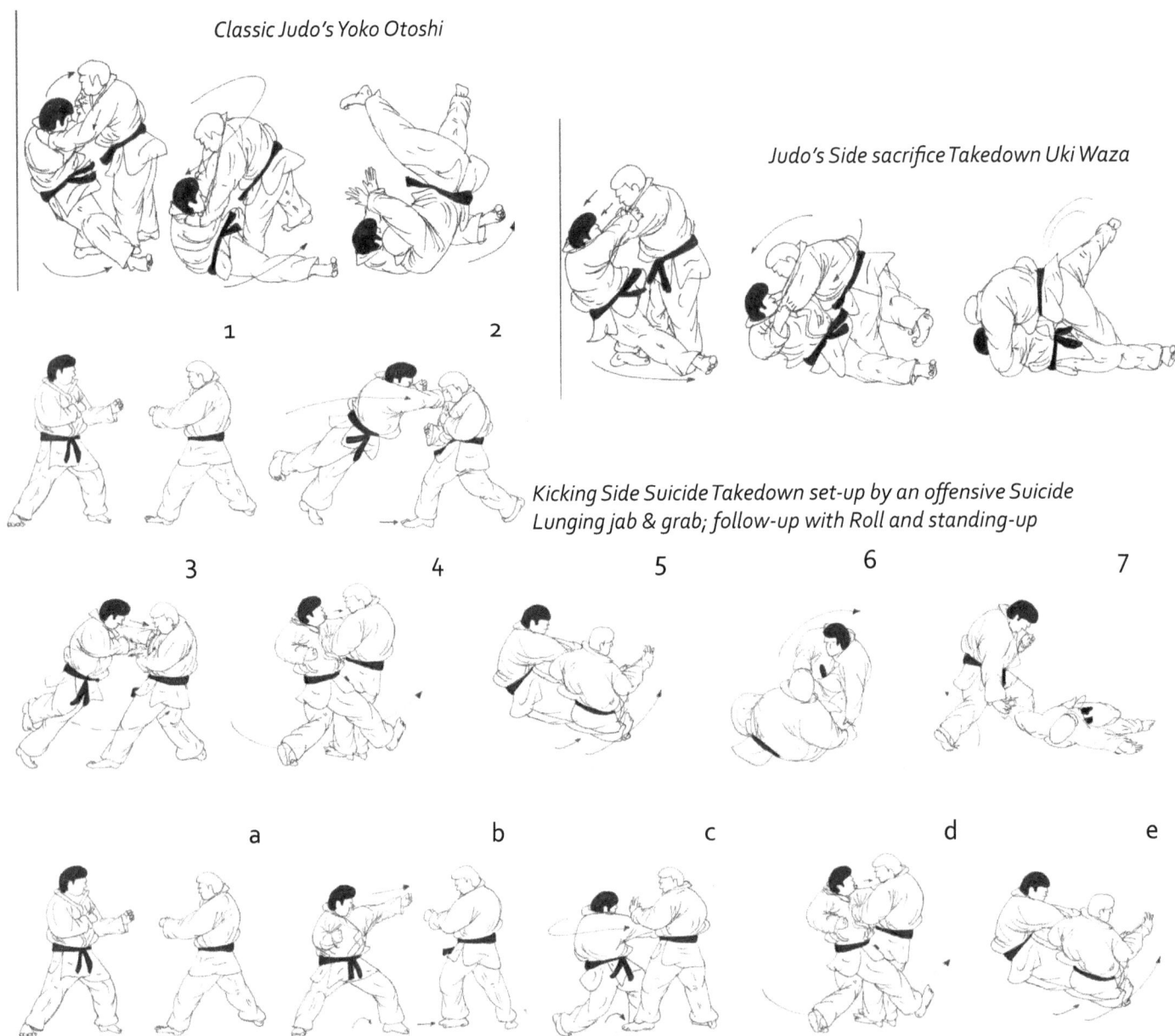

1   2

Judo's Side sacrifice Takedown Uki Waza

Kicking Side Suicide Takedown set-up by an offensive Suicide Lunging jab & grab; follow-up with Roll and standing-up

3   4   5   6   7

a   b   c   d   e

Open with classic lunging Reverse Punch, whether offensive or defensive; follow-up with kicking Suicide Takedown

43. THE FRONT KICK TO BACK CARTWHEEL ESCAPE

General

This is not really a *Suicide Kick*, but more of a regular Kick followed by a suicidal escape. It is a typical *Capoeira* maneuver, acrobatic to the extreme. We present it because, in a simplified version, it can be an interesting escape or a worthy going-down-to-the-ground technique, that should surprise the opponent and leave him unsure of what to do. In fact, the easier and simplified Backward Roll maneuver is found in some *Ninjitsu* styles.

Description

The Illustrations below show the classic *Capoeira* move: You deliver a full-power *Penetrating Front Kick*, pushing the hips strongly forward *and not chambering back*. From this position, you exaggerate the back leaning, and then bend back until your hand gets to the floor. You simultaneously lift the kicking leg and then the other one into a **Back Cartwheel**. The author finds this version overly 'flourishy', but it is in line with *Capoeira* training style and a very good drill as well. It is a very surprising and effective escape if you are proficient.

The Front Kick to Back Cartwheel Escape, Capoeira-style

Typical Application

The Figures below show what is probably the more practical version of this technique: from the *Penetrating Front Kick*, you throw yourself back directly into a full Judo Back Roll (*Ushiro Ukemi*). As your opponent feels over-confident and 'runs' after you, you suddenly stop-kick him in the groin (See previous work about '*Ground Kicks'* and '*Stop Kicks'*).

An applied simpler version of this **Escape Kick**

I'd rather attempt to do something great and fail than to attempt to do nothing and succeed.
~Robert H. Schuller

44. THE FLYING ASSISTED STOMP KICK

General

This is a spectacular and **very effective** technique, to be used when you need to close the distance quickly, for example against an opponent wielding a long blunt weapon. It can also be a 'surprise' tactic as it is highly unexpected. This 'Suicide' technique is to be executed *fully committed* and, as such, it can be dangerous to execute: you could impale yourself on a stop-punch, a sweep, or worse. But it is a very powerful technique, easy to master and quite difficult to deal with. I love it, though it must be used parsimoniously. *Surprise* remains the key word.
We shall present directly relevant applications, as it is not really relevant out of contest.

Typical Application

The Illustrations below present a classical exercise. It shows how you evade rearwards the large swing of a Long Staff (*Bo – BoJitsu*). As soon as the staff swings by you and is carried further by its momentum, you *jump off both feet* into an **airborne** Side Neck Hold of your opponent. You jump diagonally towards his back. **Using his body as support**, you twist in the air to land behind him, still holding his neck. Your other hands should use his shoulder, his back or his lower back as support. **You land while delivering a Side Stomp Kick** to the back of his knee, so adding the power of gravity to both your own weight and the power of the Kick. You can then use the momentum to twist and go down with him while securing the Neck Lock or the Naked Choke. This is a wicked and overpowering technique that can be used in a multitude of situations. The long stick could be a chair or a baseball bat, the adversary could be unarmed but swinging wildly, or rushing you... It can even be an offensive or pre-emptive attack based on the surprising jump forward. The reader who likes the kick is invited to experiment; he will be surprised by the versatility of this maneuver.

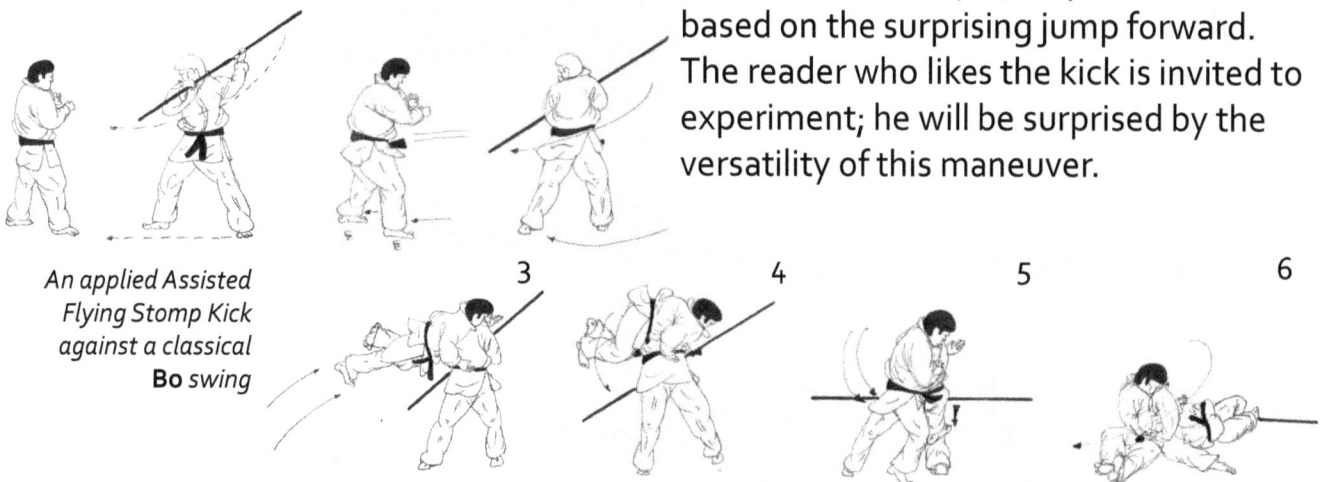

An applied Assisted Flying Stomp Kick against a classical **Bo** *swing*

Specific training

- Practice the jump from further and further away, catching a *partner's* shoulders for support and landing behind him.
- Drill the *long Forward Judo Rolls*.
- Do lots of *rope skipping* for strengthening the calves and the ability to explode forward.
- Drill *Plyometric* exercises for jump improvement.

Self defense

The Illustrations below show a variant of the technique against an opponent holding a short stick. And, this time, the Stomp Kick will be an **Outward-tilted Front Stomp Kick**. As your threatening assailant suddenly lifts his stick to gather the momentum necessary to hit you, you *jump* onto him instead of cowering back as he expects. It is all about surprise and unexpectedness. You use his body as *support* while you are *airborne*, and so you can *twist* and land directly on his back knee in an Outward-tilted Stomp Kick. Follow up either by keeping control of his neck or by keeping your Stomp in place. This is, again, a devastating technique. Caution is warranted.

Variation of the Assisted Flying Stomp Kick as a pre-emptive attack

45. OTHER SUICIDE KICKS

Here come a few *anecdotic* kicks, mostly from East Asian Arts. These are, in the author's opinion, overly dangerous or unnecessarily spectacular. There are many more, and this is just to whet the appetite of the reader. This is in no way a denigration of the Arts sporting those kinds of maneuvers, but these Kicks are out of the realm of universal kicks suitable for all Artists. For those training in these special styles, these are absolutely valid techniques, and with the added advantage of utmost unexpectedness. We just present them in an Application, for completeness and illustration. Here they come; enjoy!

Evade out and forward, Suicide Roundhouse Kick, Suicide Spin-back Hook Kick, Leg Scissor Kick, Leg Lock Submission

Evading a Reverse Punch by bending sideways, Hand-on-floor Circular Knee Stop Kick turning into Bent-over Downward Roundhouse Kick. In the Muay Boran version of this technique, one hand goes to control the rear leg of the assailant, as illustrated

Feet straight to the midsection, knees to the face, elbows to the top of the head. Even if catches your legs automatically, you have already scored hard

Outward-tilted Front Stop Kick against Reverse Punch, turning into Assisted Roundhouse Flying Kick

The opponent "checks" you up with prodding Front Kicks. Stop-kick his next attempt with a rear-leg Flying Side Kick over the attacking limb

Your opponent 'prods' you with rear-leg Low Kicks and gets used to your leg-blocks. You pre-empt the next one by jumping onto him, striking his chest with your pelvis, his head with your fists and his sides with your inside knees. You land while twisting in something akin to a Flying Hand-on-floor Downward Roundhouse Kick

184   **SACRIFICE KICKS**

AFTERWORD

AFTERWORD

We have come to the end of our imperfect research about *Flying Kicks* and *Suicide Kicks*. As mentioned many times, it should be clear to the reader that this book presents a certain classification and a certain outlook that is by no means absolute. This is the way the author feels about Sacrifice-Kicking, in a general way suited to his experience and morphology.

In no way should the reader feel that this is an orthodox presentation set in stone. It should be, in my eyes, the basis for a personal exploration and research suited to each Artist in its own way. As said by one of my betters:

Always be yourself, express yourself, have faith in yourself, do not go out and look for a successful personality and duplicate it. ~Bruce Lee

The reader is invited to try to execute the Kicks described here in the spirit in which they are presented. The reader is supposed to be a practicing Martial Artist and will have no problem to execute the techniques presented, as they are combinations and/or variations of regular *basic* techniques

The reader should then try to drill the applications presented, both in the **Applications** and in the **Self-defense** sections. Some of those combinations may seem far-fetched or inappropriate to some readers, because it does not align with their style, because the way free-fighting is regulated in their art/sport, or because they do not "believe" in it. The author begs you to drill these applications anyway: the body should be subjected to all possible situations and possible ways to fight, even if the specific technique would not be used willfully by the trainee. Just like mental intuition is in fact based on a long experience at the **subconscious** level, real fighting is done *automatically* by your body and by your unconscious mind, based on all the experience gathered in training. You never know when your body will decide, in the fight, that a certain "new" reaction is the right thing to do. You can plan a general tactic before a fight, but once in the fire of the action, it is your unconscious that will react: if you would have to think about your reaction to every specific strike, you would be in serious trouble. Therefore, you must feed "data" to your body and mind, by drilling time and again all sorts of combinations, techniques, reactions, positioning, and more.

And try not to judge harshly other styles and other ways of fighting than your own school: you can never really know. Not everything in your style or not everything working for you is necessarily the best for others. Among the comments I received after the publication of 'The Essential Book of Martial Arts Kicks', was from a reader that did not agree to the use of a Drop Kick presented as an application against a mugger in the Self-Defense section. Why go to the ground against a mugger? Although I personally would not have used this particular technique, it is certainly valid if used by some artists like Capoeira practitioners, MMA ground fighters, some Indonesian stylists and many more. You could find yourself on the ground by accident too! I have had the greatest difficulty in handling ground fighters myself, and I would not be quick to judge any technique. I implore the reader to keep things in perspective, to be respectful of the emphasis of other styles and to try everything. And to keep an open mind…Hubris has caused many downfalls…

Suicide Kicks, as we have named them here, are an important part of the Art of Kicking. All Artists should experiment with them, whether they feel it is suitable to their morphologies or not. It is important to be able to gauge one's abilities in context, and this can only be achieved by *serious training*. Later, each individual will feel which techniques are well adapted to his affinities, to his morphology and to his personality. Some could be surprised; I have seen it many times!

It is clear that *Jumping Kicks* are not the ideal maneuvers for certain morphologies, but some versions can be a worthwhile addition to your own arsenal.
On the other hand, Jumping and Suicide Kicks are techniques extremely well suited to others. And the Kicks presented should all be tried by such Artists who could then choose their preferred ones for further training and investigation.

The author, although he used *Flying Kicks* in combat in his early competitive career, is rather endomorphic and not especially suitably-built for the extensive use of Flying Kicks. This book has tried to distil the Flying Kicks theory with the widest common denominator for all stylists and all body types. Our 'Kicks' series would not be complete without a serious treatment of the Airborne Kicks. The trained reader realizes easily that there is much more to Flying Kicks than what is described herein; whoever has had his appetite whetted by this book, should definitely go further and specialize.

The *Ectomorphic* fighters, small and light, should definitely become proficient with **Flying Kicks**. They, and other enthusiasts, are invited to consult further literature on the subject. It is clear that the most interesting styles for those interested are the **Korean** styles like *TaeKwonDo, TangSooDo, HwaRangDo, Taekkyeon, Hapkido* and the like. Those styles and schools are working hard on Jumping and Flying Kicks and drill them in many specific ways. Their competitive fighting rules encourage the use of these difficult techniques and teach the trainees how to use them for real and to set them up. The interested reader is warmly invited to join a Korean Art school and to check the literature concerning those styles. Then start drilling, drilling and drilling:

We are what we repeatedly do. Excellence then, is not an act, but a habit.
~ Aristotle

The fans of **Suicide Kicks** would be better served by practicing *Capoeira*, for its spectacular and sneaky techniques. Capoeiristas hover close to the ground in constant movement; they cartwheel around, feint and then whirl into redoubtable acrobatic kicks. The whole style is based on deception, misdirection and the effect of surprise. Readers are invited to join such a school, research the subject further, and then adapt the principles and techniques to their own style and morphologies. As we have hammered in our previous book about 'Stealth Kicks', the difference between a good technique and a great technique is making it undetected until it is too late. Surprise is a key weapon in you arsenal. And Suicide techniques are definitely *surprising*!

Who overcomes by force, hath overcome but half his foe.
~ John Milton

And Please remember that the fact that our Book Series has cataloged a great number of Kicks does not mean that you have to know and master them all. As already mentioned, a good Martial Artist must first master the basics of his chosen style by hard work on the Essential techniques. Only when he has done so, should he try advanced maneuvers and special techniques from other Arts. He should then drill new and unconventional techniques, and then try them in free fighting. A real Artist will then know how to choose only a few techniques that are suitable to his morphology, psychology and liking. These very few techniques will then have to be drilled for thousands and thousands of times until they become natural. During the fight, it is the body that intuitively choses the best technique to be used. If you have to think about what to do, you have already lost! The expected relevant quote follows: ➤

I fear not the man who has practiced 10,000 kicks once, but I fear the man who has practiced one kick 10,000 times.
~ Bruce Lee

And now, dear reader, what is left is for you to start sweating.
And a quote by a Fly-kicking Korean Art personality is certainly appropriate:

Pain is the best instructor, but no one wants to go to his class.
~Choi, Hong Hi, Founder of Taekwon-Do

If you have enjoyed the book and appreciate the effort behind this series, you are invited to write a short honest review on Amazon.com...It has become extremely difficult to promote one's work in this day and age, and your support would be much appreciated. Thanks!

All questions, comments, additional techniques, special or vintage Photos about Suicide Kicks, or other Kicks, are welcomed by the author and would be introduced with credit in future editions. Just email:**martialartkicks@gmail.com**

The author is trying to build a complete series of work that, once finished, could become an encyclopedic base of the whole of the Martial Arts-Kicking realm, a base on which others could build and add their own experiences.

In his endeavors the author has already penned:

- **The Essential Book of Martial Arts Kicks** – *Tuttle Publishing* (2010)
- **Plyo-Flex** - Training for Explosive Martial Arts Kicks (2013)
- **Low Kicks** - Advanced Martial Arts Kicks for Attacking the Lower Gates (2013)
- **Stop Kicks** – Jamming, Obstructing, Stopping, Impaling, Cutting and Preemptive Kicks (2014)
- **Ground Kicks** – Advanced Martial Arts Kicks for groundfighting (2015)
- **Stealth Kicks** - The Forgotten Art of Ghost Kicking (2015)

In the same frame of mind, the following works are in preparation:

- Combo Kicks
- Krav Maga Kicks
- Joint Kicks

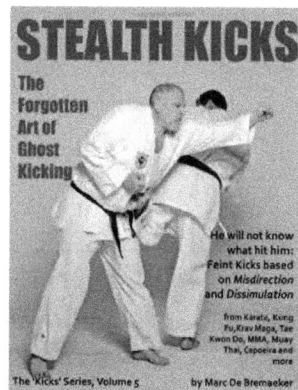

Only one who devotes himself to a cause with his whole strength and soul can be a true master. For this reason mastery demands all of a person.
~Albert Einstein

LOW KICKS

Advanced Martial Arts Kicks for Attacking the Lower Gates

A Comprehensive Study of the Art of Realistic Kicking Below the Belt

by MARC DE BREMAEKER

Low Kicks are powerful, fast, and effective exactly what you need to defend yourself in a real life confrontation. And because they are seldom used in sport fighting, they can be a surprising and valuable addition to your free fighting arsenal. While they may seem easy to execute, not all low kicks are simply low versions of the basic kicks. There are specific attributes and principles that make low kicks work. Marc de Bremaeker has collected the most effective low kicking techniques from Martial Arts like *Krav Maga, Karatedo, Capoeira, Wing-Chun Kung-Fu, MMA,* and *Muay Thai.* In this book, he analyzes each kick in depth, explaining the proper execution and outlining applications and variations from self-defense, sport fighting and traditional practice: Hundreds of examples in over one thousand photographs and drawings.

PLYO-FLEX

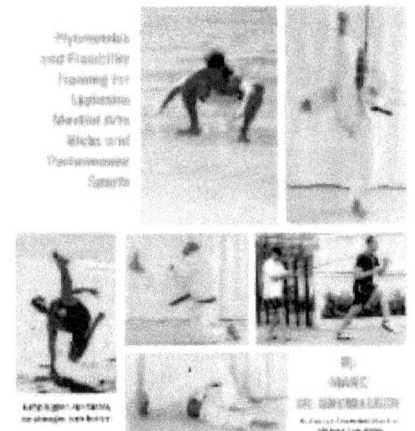

Plyometrics and Flexibility Training for Explosive Martial Arts Kicks and Performance Sports Plyo-Flex is a system of plyometric exercises and intensive flexibility training designed to increase your kicking power, speed, flexibility and skill level. Based on scientific principles, Plyo-Flex exercises will boost your muscles, joints and nervous system interfaces to the next performance level. After only a few weeks of training, you should see a marked improvement in the speed of your kicks and footwork, the power of your kicks, the height of your jumps, your stamina and your overall flexibility. Hundreds of illustrations and photographs will guide you through the basic plyometric and stretching exercises. Once you've mastered the basics, add the kicking-oriented variations to your workout for an extra challenge.

STOP KICKS

Jamming, Obstructing, Stopping, Impaling, Cutting and Preemptive Kicks

by MARC DE BREMAEKER

Stop Kicks are among the most effective, sophisticated kicks a fighter can use. And because they hit your opponent at his most vulnerable, they are also the safest way to pre-empt or counter an attack. Stop Kicks are delivered just as your opponent is fully committed to an attack, physically or mentally, meaning it is too late for him to change his mind. Hitting an opponent in mid-attack gives you the added advantage of using his attacking momentum against him. Stop Kicks: Jamming, Obstructing, Stopping, Impaling, Cutting and Preemptive Kicks presents a well organized array of stop-kicking techniques from a wide range of martial arts. Learn Pushing Kicks, Timing Kicks, Cutting Kicks, Obstruction Kicks, and Block Kicks from the hard-hitting styles of Muay Thai, Karatedo, Krav Maga, Tae Kwon Do, MMA and more.

Whether you are on the ground by choice or you have been taken down, whether your opponent is standing or is on the ground with you, whether you are a good grappler or you are trying to keep a good grappler at bay, whether you were caught unawares sitting on the floor or you have evaded down on purpose, whether you are a beginner or an experienced martial artist...this book has the right kick for the situation. In **Ground Kicks**: Advanced Martial Arts Kicks for Ground-fighting from Karate, Krav Maga, MMA, Capoeira, Kung Fu and more, Marc De Bremaeker has created a comprehensive collection of Ground Kicks, with hundreds of applications for sport fighting and self-defense situation. Packed with over 1200 photographs and illustrations, Ground Kicks also includes specific training tips for practicing each kick effectively.

GROUND KICKS

Advanced Martial Arts Kicks for Groundfighting

Ne Gari Waza - The Art of Fighting from Down Under

by MARC DE BREMAEKER
Author of Stop Kicks and Low Kicks

With hundreds of applications from Karate, Krav Maga, MMA, Capoeira, Kung Fu and more

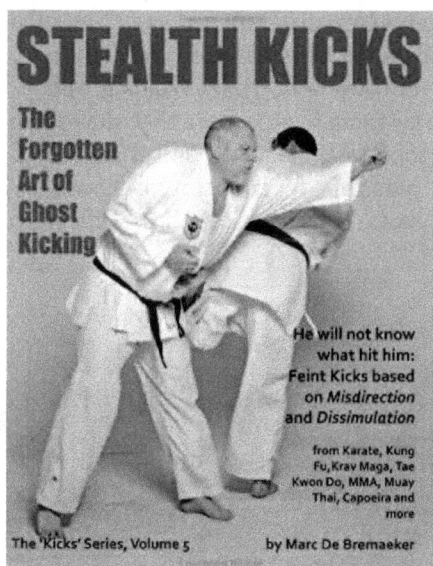

STEALTH KICKS

The Forgotten Art of Ghost Kicking

He will not know what hit him: Feint Kicks based on *Misdirection* and *Dissimulation*

from Karate, Kung Fu, Krav Maga, Tae Kwon Do, MMA, Muay Thai, Capoeira and more

The 'Kicks' Series, Volume 5   by Marc De Bremaeker

Stealth Kicks will introduce you to the Art of executing Kicks that your opponent will not see coming. This subject has never been treated comprehensively before. Whether you are a beginner or an experienced Artist, you will find suitable Kicks or tips to modify your current techniques to give them stealth. It will help you to score in Sport confrontations or make sure to come on top in real life Self-Defense situations. The *Feint Kicks* presented are based on misdirection: they will aim at provoking a misguided reaction that will open your adversary to the real kick intended. The *Ghost Kicks* presented are based on dissimulation and will travel out of your opponent's range of vision to catch him unawares.
Together with general feinting techniques and specific training tips, hundreds of applications will introduce you to the sneaky Art of stealth kicking and will make you a better and unpredictable fighter. Crammed with over 2300 photos and drawings for an easy understanding of the concept of Stealth.

Perfection is not attainable, but if we chase perfection we can catch excellence.
~Vince Lombardi

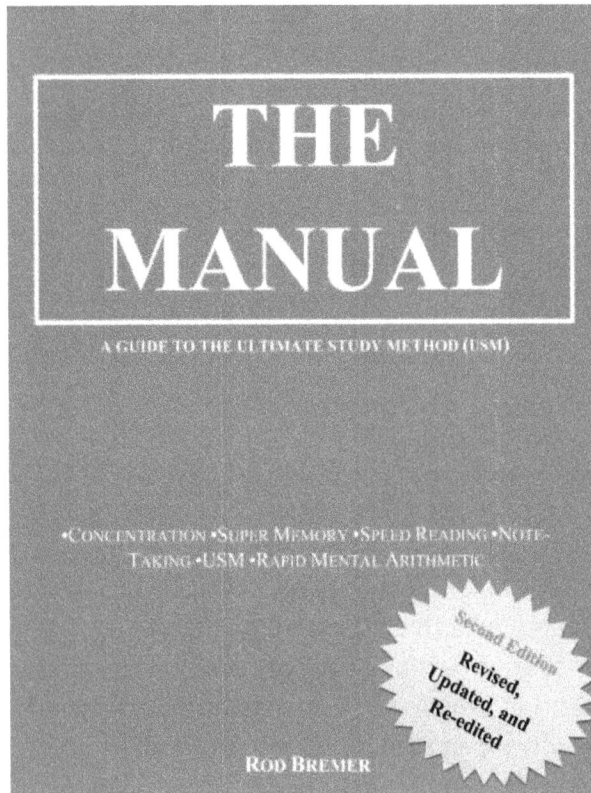

The Manual is the definitive guide to Enhanced Concentration, Super Memory, Speed Reading, Note-Taking, Rapid Mental Arithmetic, and the *Ultimate Study Method* (USM).

The techniques presented are the culmination of decades of practical experience combined with the latest scientific research and time-tested practices. The system described herewith will allow the practitioner to:

• Read faster with higher comprehension.
• Remember any type of information instantly.
• Store information in long-term memory.
• Enhance concentration and focus.
• Access deeper levels of the mind.
• Induce relaxation.
• Rapidly perform complex mental arithmetic.
• Master the Ultimate Study Method (USM).

USM is a synergistic combination of established techniques for Concentration, Long-Term Memory, Speed Reading, and Note-Taking. It involves a systematic procedure that allows the practitioner to study any topic fast, efficiently and effectively. USM can be applied to all areas of educational study, academic research, business endeavours, as well as professional life in general.

Rain Fund: A riveting thriller

"...For the safety of the readers, this book ought to come with the disclaimer: leave this book read half-way at your own risk. Unless you are Superman, you won't be able to concentrate on much else until you have read the last page of "Rain Fund". The time has come for Patterson, Ludlum, Dan Brown et al to slide over and make space at the top for Marc Brem." - Shweta Shankar for Readers' Favorite

"...In the good tradition of Ludlum and Grisham. Five Stars" Aldo Levy

"Autistic geniuses charting financial markets; Mobster-fuelled Ponzi schemes; sophisticated hardware viruses; spies; and a rising superpower that strives for dominance – so realistic it is frightening."

SACRIFICE KICKS